D0142635

CAMBRIDGE   MUSIC   HANDBOOKS

Vivaldi: *The Four Seasons* and other concertos, Op. 8

CAMBRIDGE MUSIC HANDBOOKS

GENERAL EDITOR Julian Rushton

Cambridge Music Handbooks provide accessible introductions to major musical works, written by the most informed commentators in the field.

With the concert-goer, performer and student in mind, the books present essential information on the historical and musical context, the composition, and the performance and reception history of each work, or group of works, as well as critical discussion of the music.

Other published titles

Vivaldi: *The Four Seasons* and other concertos, Op. 8

Paul Everett

CAMBRIDGE
UNIVERSITY PRESS

Published by the Press Syndicate of the University of Cambridge
The Pitt Building, Trumpington Street, Cambridge CB2 1RP
40 West 20th Street, New York, NY 10011–4211, USA
10 Stamford Road, Oakleigh, Melbourne 3166, Australia

First published 1996

Printed in Great Britain at the University Press, Cambridge

A catalogue record for this book is available from the British Library

Library of Congress cataloguing in publication data
Everett, Paul.
Vivaldi, The Four Seasons and other concertos, Op. 8 / Paul Everett
p. cm. – (Cambridge Music Handbooks)
Includes bibliographical references (p.) and index.
ISBN 0 521 40499 1 (hardback) – ISBN 0 521 40692 7 (paperback)
1. Vivaldi, Antonio, 1678–1741. Cimento dell'armonia e dell'inventione.
I. Title. II. Series.
ML410.V82E84 1996
784.2'72–dc20 95–18173 CIP M

ISBN 0 521 40499 1 hardback
ISBN 0 521 40692 7 paperback

AH

To Marg and Martin

Contents

Contents

Illustrations

These pages are reproduced by kind permission of the libraries concerned.

Preface

Considerable significance has attached to Antonio Vivaldi's *opera ottava*, the eighth set of his instrumental pieces to be published during his lifetime. As well as being cited as a landmark in the history of programme music, *The Four Seasons* alone have borne and still bear heavy responsibility as the composer's most well-known, most admired and most frequently performed works. For many people, the very name 'Vivaldi' is synonymous with *The Four Seasons* to the exclusion of all else. The phenomenon of the *Seasons* has had its advantages: a guaranteed audience for concerts, a reliable market for recordings, and a high public profile that has underpinned the rapid progress, since the 1940s, of research into and performance of the rest of the composer's music. From those advantages (for which the present writer is most grateful) benefits such as a niche for Vivaldi in the Cambridge Handbooks' series continue to be reaped. The disadvantage was that knowledge of the composer's life, works and stylistic development, even among musicians whose interests lay primarily in Baroque repertory, remained scant and distinctly unbalanced with a *Seasons*-heavy tilt. That tilt is no longer as steep as it was, now that performers and musicologists are demonstrating a much greater appreciation of the wide variety in style and function of Vivaldi's concertos and beginning to grasp the breadth of his whole output.

In the past, a concentration on Op. 8 in critical literature was inevitable. Before research began in earnest on the huge number of extant autograph manuscripts (preserved mainly in Turin and Dresden),[1] knowledge of Vivaldi's concertos was largely confined to the collections printed in the eighteenth century, from which Op. 8 stands out as the composer's most idiosyncratic compilation. Even after many other concertos had become known from manuscript sources, scholars continued to draw attention, rightly so, to the special nature of *The Four Seasons* – but they also had little option but to rely heavily on Op. 8 for another important reason. Since virtually all Vivaldi's manuscripts bear no date and seemed to be undatable, the publication-date of Op. 8 (1725) remained the only *terminus ante quem* for his maturity in concerto composition and his use of allusive titles.

That limitation no longer exists; approximate dating of many of the manuscripts has recently been found to be both possible and immensely illuminating. For this reason, and in recognition of other advances in scholarship that bear on Vivaldi's status today, the time is ripe for a re-evaluation of Op. 8 in a way that is not shackled to conclusions drawn in the past. We are now better placed than ever before to locate the collection in a broad context and to assess the significance of its richly varied music. Any attempt to do this cannot address Op. 8 in isolation as if its music were cocooned by virtue of its first publication. Somewhat inconveniently, the collection is not a single, integrated conception but rather a selection of individual compositions that are as likely to have points in common with concertos outside the set as they are likely to relate to each other.

Ultimately, a full account of the actions and thoughts of composers, especially those born over three centuries ago, cannot be made. The present book raises as many questions as it provides answers, and gaps in the evidence currently available keep certain conclusions at the level of hypothesis. Vivaldi's methods and motivations in concerto-design, allusive labelling and the packaging of works in sets will continue to be pondered, and the collection's title, 'The Trial of Harmony and Invention', will remain the trial of the programme-note writer's skill that it has always been.

For their kind assistance I thank many friends and colleagues, particularly Roger-Claude Travers, Carlo Vitali, Yolanda Plumley, Mark Chu for translating Italian texts and Antonio Fanna for granting access to the archive of the Istituto Italiano Antonio Vivaldi (Fondazione Cini, Venice). I am especially indebted to Julian Rushton for his encouragement and patience over several years, and to Michael Talbot for his generous advice. To my wife and son, who have supported me and suffered while I worked, I owe both thanks and an apology. This book is dedicated to them, with love.

A note on editions and recordings

Various modern editions of *The Four Seasons* (Op. 8 Nos. 1–4) exist, but it must be said that their texts are invariably inaccurate in some respects. New critical editions will be published in 1996 by Ricordi (Milan); based on the earliest edition of Op. 8, they will also record the variants of the manuscripts preserved in Manchester (see p. 11). Op. 8 Nos. 5–12 are far less accessible, almost all being available only in the editions prepared by Gian Francesco

Malipiero and Angelo Ephrikian, published as separate volumes by Ricordi in 1947–50. By today's editorial standards, these texts leave much to be desired, though they are serviceable if one ignores their invented double bass parts. (Incorrect Ricordi readings that impinge on our discussion are explained, as they arise, in the notes at the end of the book.) The cheapest solution for readers requiring all twelve concertos of Op. 8 is to obtain the Ricordi editions in miniature score: two volumes, PR 1235–6, available in Britain from Novello. (See the note on bar numbers, p. xiv.)

The earliest edition of Op. 8 (Amsterdam, 1725) is published in facsimile by Alamire (Peer, Belgium, 1990). In separate parts, it is of interest particularly to performers.

Since a regularly updated Vivaldi discography is published elsewhere (see Chapter 1, note 2), it will suffice to recommend some outstanding recordings issued in recent years. Undoubtedly the best interpretation of Op. 8 in its entirety is that of Monica Huggett (violin) with The Raglan Baroque Players directed by Nicholas Kraemer (1990: Virgin VCD 790803–2). Excellent performances of *The Four Seasons* alone include those by Jeanne Lamon (violin and director) with Tafelmusik (1992: Sony CD SK 48307); various soloists with The Taverner Players directed by Andrew Parrott (1990: EMI CD CDC 7 54208–2); and, playing the Manchester texts, Simon Standage (violin) with The English Concert directed by Trevor Pinnock (1981: Archiv DG 2534.003).

1   The bulk of them, constituting Vivaldi's own collection that remained in his possession until his death in 1741, was recovered from private ownership and acquired by the National Library, Turin, in 1927–30. Marc Pincherle's *Antonio Vivaldi et la musique instrumentale* (Paris, 1948) was the first major study to benefit from access to them. The full extent of their riches became evident only in the 1970s following the cataloguing work of Peter Ryom (see p. xiv).

Abbreviations

RV   'Répertoire Vivaldi': work-numbers as given in P. Ryom, *Répertoire des Œuvres d'Antonio Vivaldi. Les compositions instrumentales* (Copenhagen, 1986) and – for vocal compositions – the same writer's *Verzeichnis der Werke Antonio Vivaldis: kleine Ausgabe* (Leipzig, 1974; 2nd edn, 1979).

ISV   *Informazioni e studi vivaldiani*, annual bulletin of the Istituto Italiano Antonio Vivaldi (Fondazione Cini, Venice), published by Ricordi (Milan, 1980–).

Library sigla

D-Dlb	Dresden, Sächsische Landesbibliothek
D-SWl	Schwerin, Mecklenburgische Landesbibliothek
F-Pn	Paris, Bibliothèque Nationale
GB-Mp	Manchester, Central Library, Henry Watson Music Library
I-Gi(l)	Genoa, Istituto Musicale, Biblioteca del Liceo Musicale 'Paganini'
I-Tn	Turin, Biblioteca Nazionale Universitaria
S-L	Lund, Universitetsbiblioteket

Bar references

The Ricordi editions (to which, it is assumed, most readers will refer) number bars continuously through the three movements of a concerto. This difficulty is taken into account in the present book. Thus 'bars 63–78/144–59 in the finale', for example, refers to the finale's actual bars 63–78 reckoned by Ricordi as 144–59.

One collection, two Vivaldis

The popularity of *Le quattro staggioni* (*The Four Seasons*) still knows no bounds. Having reached a kind of critical mass, it now seems to reproduce itself every year or two. Other compositions from Western art-music traditions have found their way to popular culture and to the dubious status of 'classical pops', but not to such a widespread extent. The easy acceptance of the *Seasons* by many persons not devotees of classical music can in part be attributed to the timelessness and appeal of the music itself, but causes other than the excellence of Vivaldi's conception must be acknowledged. Credit for creating a Vivaldi phenomenon in our generation is due as much to the media and the recording industry as to musicians, concert promoters and musicologists.

Snatches of the *Seasons* are indelibly etched on the consciousness of whole populations across the world, thanks largely to the commercial astuteness of directors of advertising who hear in the music a heady mix of outdoor freshness, nostalgia for times past and an Italian modishness that is as potent for marketing purposes as claiming that the product is made in Milan. This awareness of 'Vivaldi' – as opposed to a familiarity, shared by relatively few people, with a range of Vivaldi's works – was made inevitable by the astonishing proliferation of LP and CD recordings of the *Seasons*. The tally of recorded interpretations issued since Bernardino Molinari's version appeared on 78-rpm records in 1942, now over 200,[1] is evidence of the extraordinary value, artistic and financial, placed on these works by performers and record companies alike. That proliferation peaked in the 1980s as modern-instrument ensembles and their recording managers strove to retain their market share against the highly successful encroachment of original-instrument versions. From 1987 to 1990, recordings of the *Seasons* in one form or another, including arrangements and re-releases, appeared at an average rate of nineteen per year. Because it pays dividends, the tradition is well entrenched: since the 1950s virtually every solo violinist, every conductor and every orchestra have aspired to issue at least one recording both as evidence of their respective interpretative skills and as a mark of professional status. Others, over the years, have climbed upon the *Seasons*' bandwagon with recorded performances of arranged versions, for combinations ranging from the mildly odd (trombone and strings, brass quintet, flute and accordion, etc.) to the vividly esoteric (six *koto* – a Japanese type of psaltery; three synthesizers, violin and orchestra; etc.).[2]

There are, then, two Vivaldis with distinct audiences. One is the Vivaldi of popular and somewhat mythical conception, based exclusively on exposure to *The Four Seasons* and the treatment of those works either as test pieces or fair game for 'creative' arrangement. The other is the true Vivaldi revealed only by a wider range of his works – including the *Seasons*, which deservedly occupy a central and significant position. The problem of reconciling the two Vivaldis is the underlying theme of the present book. The Op. 8 collection itself presents the problem in a nutshell since it juxtaposes the *Seasons* with eight other concertos with which only a small minority of potential readers will be familiar. And yet it conveniently offers the solution, too, because an understanding of either one of these sub-sets informs an understanding of the other – and neither can properly be understood in isolation.

Was it ever thus? In a way, yes – for Vivaldi himself was responsible for making the *Seasons* stand apart, in both presentation and substance, from other concertos including his own. It is hardly surprising that they were singled out for special attention when his music came to be rescued from oblivion – a process that began only in the present century.[3] The modern tendency for performers to arrange the music in personalized interpretations was set in motion by those who championed the rediscovery itself, partly because the invention of some kind of performance practice was justified in the absence of knowledge of the actual practices of the past, and partly because the functions of transcription and freely creative performance were inseparably entangled in the minds of influential artists such as Ottorino Respighi and Fritz Kreisler.[4] The earliest 'modern' editions (from 1908) of works by Vivaldi, with their invented harmonies, orchestrations and piano accompaniments, set in train a tradition of less-than-faithful transcription that persisted in the house style of Ricordi of Milan.[5] Traces of it have come down to us in the *Opere strumentali* (Ricordi, 1947–72), which for hundreds of works remains the only edition available today.[6]

In some respects, twentieth-century attitudes towards the *Seasons* seem uncannily to pick up where eighteenth-century tradition left off. The historical trend towards the insulation of these works from the rest of Vivaldi's output began as soon as the music entered the public domain with the first publication of Op. 8 by the firm of Michel-Charles Le Cène (Amsterdam, 1725). (We leave description of the print itself, and of other sources, to Chapter 2.) It was not long, either, before the *Seasons* came regularly to be treated as test pieces by leading violinists and appropriated for arrangement by those succumbing to Vivaldi fever. All these factors are clear from developments in France where there was a substantial following for Vivaldi, especially at the height, from the 1730s, of the fashionable craze for Italian instrumental music.[7]

Op. 8, and the *Seasons* in particular, did much to enhance Vivaldi's fame in France but did not actually create it. A published compliment, quoted below, strongly hints that his reputation, in Paris at least, was already remarkably high a few months before Op.8 was first advertised in December 1725.[8] The reasons for this are not entirely clear but probably have much to do with the success of his earlier publications in northern Europe and his indirect association with the French crown via the occasional patronage of Jacques-Vincent Languet, comte de Gergy, from 1723 the French Ambassador to Venice.[9] In October 1725 the *Mercure de France* reported extensively on the entertainment given at the ambassador's residence on 12 September in celebration of the marriage (5 September) between Louis XV and Princess Maria Leszczyńska, at which was performed a serenata (RV 687, 'Dall'eccelsa mia reggia') by Vivaldi, *le plus habile compositeur qui soit à Venise* – 'the most accomplished composer in Venice'.[10]

Royal approval of Vivaldi is also implicit in the fact that *La primavera* (*Spring*) was played at the French monarch's court on 25 November 1730 by a band containing members of the nobility.[11] This performance, however, was probably more a response to public fashion than a catalyst for it, for the roll and frequency of works performed at the Concert Spirituel show that *Spring* was by then fast becoming the most admired concerto in Parisian musical life.[12] The earliest known performances of Vivaldi's music in that series show a narrowing of focus: *The Four Seasons* as a set (7 February 1728); *Spring* and *Summer* (4–5 April 1728); *Spring* alone (21 February 1729). After that initial phase there is a gap of seven years before the next recorded appearance of a Vivaldi work – a lull, one supposes, before the Vivaldi cult was revitalized by publications, discussed below. *Summer*, *Autumn* and *Winter* make no further appearance at the Concert Spirituel; *Spring* is the work played on eleven out of the sixteen pertinent occasions during the period 1736–63, with one outing for *La tempesta di mare* (Op. 8 No. 5) in 1749 and four unidentified Vivaldi concertos making up the remainder. These details show too that *Spring* was the recurring vehicle for the virtuosity of many of the foremost violinists of the age, both French and Italian, including Jean-Pierre Guignon (a pupil of Giovanni Battista Somis of Turin) who first championed the work in 1728 and 1729, Pierre Gaviniès at the age of thirteen (1741), and André-Noël Pagin and Domenico Ferrari, who had both studied under Tartini.

The *Seasons*, particularly *Spring*, also loom large in the sphere of Parisian publishing. Copies of Op. 8 and Vivaldi's other collections printed in Amsterdam were imported and sold by Jean-Pantaléon Le Clerc *l'aîné*, who from 1733 was Le Cène's official agent in Paris. Between 1736 and 1740, his younger brother, Charles-Nicolas Le Clerc *le cadet*, published his own freshly engraved editions of several of the Amsterdam collections (including Op. 8, in 1739) having received a royal licence to do so, and various reprintings followed in the 1740s. In the face of the Le Clerc monopoly, other Parisian musicians sought different means of cashing in on an evidently lucrative market in which the name 'Vivaldi' was the richest prize. Two methods – one deceitful, the other legitimate – were adopted by Nicolas Chédeville (1705–82). Recent research has established that *Il pastor fido*, a set of six sonatas published as the 'Op. 13' of Vivaldi, is a clever musical forgery perpetrated by Chédeville with the complicity of his cousin Jean-Noël Marchand, under whose imprint and licence the collection appeared in around 1737.[13] In a further attempt to reap Vivaldian dividends while promoting his instrument (the musette), Chédeville published – under his own name and licence – *Le printems ou les saisons amusantes*: 'Concertos d'Antonio Vivaldy' set for musettes and hurdy-gurdies with accompanying parts for violin, flute and continuo (1739). The collection contains six three-movement arrangements based variously on whole concertos and reordered movements from Op. 8.[14]

Chédeville's motivation may be inferred from his choice of passages for adaptation. He was evidently at pains to exaggerate the positive, pleasurable aspects of the year by utilizing Vivaldi's *Spring*, *Autumn* and the slow movement of *Winter*. With similar logic, the whole of Op. 8 No. 6 (*Pleasure*) was pressed into service for the fifth paraphrase, 'Les plaisirs de la Saint-Martin'. By omitting entirely reference to Vivaldi's *Summer* and the fast movements of *Winter*, the arranger scrupulously avoided their uncomfortable themes of anxiety, destruction and chilling cold. Instead, he fashioned a carefree impression of summer-time for the second work ('Les plaisirs de l'été') with movements from Nos. 12 and 10 (*The Hunt*), and cobbled together 'La moisson' (Harvest) and 'L'hiver' (Winter) in a nondescript way by selecting from Nos. 7, 8 and 9. In giving pride of place to *Spring* and the joys in Vivaldi's conceptions while suppressing other elements, Chédeville's work reflects the general French attitude and parallels the public focus of the

Concert Spirituel. It agrees, moreover, with his natural inclinations: his own published compositions (*œuvres* 1–9) have titles that almost invariably combine words such as 'amusement' or 'amusante', 'galanterie' and 'champêtre'. In siphoning off the part of Vivaldi's music that was the closest to French sensibilities at a time when the *goût champêtre* was in vogue, Chédeville claimed it as French repertory.

Although the precedent was a weak one, other peculiarly French arrangements of *Spring* eventually followed: Michel Corrette's motet, *Laudate Dominum de coelis* (1765), and Jean-Jacques Rousseau's facile version, in D major, for unaccompanied flute (1775).[15] Of the two, Corrette's is by far the more interesting (despite its appallingly contrived word-setting) and an advance on Chédeville's simplistic approach, for it contains original melodies that interlace with Vivaldi's parts, vivid orchestrations (with horns) and two solo-vocal movements that were freshly composed.

In contrast, hardly any reflections of the popularity of the *Seasons* emanated from Italy. Doubtless the works came to be known and performed there widely, for in 1761 Carlo Goldoni singled them out as Vivaldi's principal claim to fame:

This most famous violinist, this man famous for his instrumental works, especially those entitled the *Four Seasons*, also composed operas; and however much connoisseurs claimed that his counterpoint was defective and that he did not set basses properly, he made his parts melodious, and his operas were most often successful.[16]

But left in ignorance of actual performances, one wonders if the *Seasons* made even the slightest impact in the composer's own environment in their early years of existence. There is a danger, of course, of reading too much into the lack of information and the paucity of surviving Italian manuscripts of the music. Performance materials and documentary evidence become lost, after all; in any case, it is exceedingly rare for the concertos played in Italy, typically at private concerts quite unlike the public Concert Spirituel, ever to be precisely identified in contemporary accounts. Nevertheless, it is just conceivable that Vivaldi kept the *Seasons* under wraps, regarding them as usable only by those consumers, whether private ones or his public north of the Alps, who would relish their special format. Did he perhaps suppress them in the face of the satirical attacks, directed at him and others responsible for Venetian opera, in Benedetto Marcello's *Il teatro alla moda* of 1720?[17] The pamphlet scorns, among other things, the over-use in arias of Nature's elements (winds, storms, fogs, ice, etc.) and inhabitants (various birds, insects, tigers, etc.). It might not be purely coincidental that the sole surviving

Venetian manuscript of the *Seasons*, apparently notated as late as 1726, was possessed by the Roman court of Cardinal Pietro Ottoboni together with other Vivaldi concertos carefully selected, by the composer himself, for their individual qualities (see p. 19). Vivaldi tended to promote his music on a tactical basis; the discernment with which he released particular works, packaging them for distinct purposes, should not be underestimated.

2

Origin and motivation

The earliest edition of Op. 8, entitled *Il cimento dell'armonia e dell'inventione*, was published in Amsterdam – probably towards the end of 1725 when, in December, it was advertised.[1] Printed from engraved plates, the music has the clear appearance that we associate with the firm of Michel-Charles Le Cène: a style more utilitarian than handsome but ideal for performance purposes (see Plate 1). The publication is particularly graced, however, by the portrait of Vivaldi engraved by François Morellon La Cave, reproduced on the cover of the present book.[2] As is customary for many eighteenth-century collections, the twelve works are divided between two volumes or 'books': *Libro primo* (Nos. 1–6), produced from plates numbered '520', and *Libro secondo* (Nos. 7–12, plate-number 521). It is equally typical that the music is presented not in score but in separate instrumental partbooks, each with its own title-page; the principal violin part of the first volume also contains a dedicatory epistle, as expected in a first edition. These texts are shown in transcription, with English translation, overleaf.[3] Transcriptions of the sonnets for *The Four Seasons* are given in Chapter 6.

Multiform patronage

Many details remain to be discovered about Vivaldi's service to the dedicatee, the Bohemian count Wenzel von Morzin or, in Czech, Václav Morzin (1676–1737): Chamberlain to the Habsburg emperor Charles VI, and distant cousin of the Morzins familiar to us as Haydn's patrons.[4] Op. 8 reveals that Vivaldi acted as the count's *maestro di musica in Italia*; in this capacity he appears to have been commissioned on an occasional basis to send fresh compositions by mail, in much the same way as Luigi Boccherini would later supply Friedrich Wilhelm II of Prussia from his base in Spain. From the dedicatory letter we learn that this relationship had existed for 'many years' – perhaps from the mid-1710s? – and that *The Four Seasons* had been received by the count and his 'most accomplished orchestra' some time ago. We know the identity of only

IL CIMENTO DELL' ARMONIA
E DELL' INVENTIONE
CONCERTI
a 4 e 5
Consacrati
ALL ILLUSTRISSIMO SIGNORE
Il Signor Venceslao Conte di Marzin, Signore Ereditario
di Hohenelbe, Lomniz, Tschista, Krzinetz, Kaunitz, Doubek,
et Sowoluska, Cameriere Attuale, e Consigliere di
S.M.C.C.
DA D. ANTONIO VIVALDI
Maestro in Italia dell' Illustris:ᵐᵒ Signor Conte Sudetto,
Maestro de' Concerti del Pio Ospitale della Pieta in Venetia,
e Maestro di Capella dà Camera di S. A. S. il Signor
Principe Filippo Langravio d'Hassia Darmistath.
OPERA OTTAVA
Libro Primo
A AMSTERDAM
Spesa di MICHELE CARLO LE CENE
Libraro.

N.° 520

ILLUSTRISSIMO SIGNORE

Pensando frà me stesso al lungo corso dè gl'anni, ne' quali godo il / segnalatissimo onore di servire à V. S. ILL.:ᵐᵃ in qualità di Maestro / di Musica in Italia, hò arossito nel considerare che non per anco le hò / datto un saggio della profonda veneratione che le professo; Ond' è che hò / risolto di stampare il presente volume per umiliarlo à piedi di V. S. ILL.:ᵐᵃ[.] / Suplico non meravigliarsi se trà questi pochi, e deboli Concerti / V. S. ILL.:ᵐᵃ troverà le quattro stagioni sino dà tanto tempo compatite / dalla Generosa Bontà di V. S. ILL.:ᵐᵃ, mà creda, che hò stimato bene / stamparle perche ad ogni Modo che siano le Stesse pure essendo queste / accresciute, oltre li Sonetti con una distintissima dichiaratione di tutte / le cose, che in esse si spiegano, sono certo, che le giungerano, come / nuove. Quivi non mi estendo à suplicare V. S. ILL.:ᵐᵃ, acciò si / compiaccia guardare con occhio di bontà le mie debolezze perche / crederei di offendere L'innata Gentilezza con la quale V. S. ILL.:ᵐᵃ / sino da tanto tempo le sà compatire. La soma Intelligenza, che / V. S. ILL.:ᵐᵃ possiede nella Musica et il Valore della di lei Virtuosissima / Orchestra mi faraño sempre vive[r] sicuro, che le mie povere fatiche / giunte che siano nelle di lei stimatissime mani goderano quel / risalto, che non meritano. Onde altro non mi resta che suplicare / V. S. ILL.:ᵐᵃ per la continuatione del di lei Generosissimo patrocinio / e perche giammai mi tolga L'onore di sempre più rassegnarmi.

DI V. S. ILL.:ᵐᵃ

Humilissimo Devotissimo
Obligatissimo Servitore
ANTONIO VIVALDI

THE TRIAL OF HARMONY
AND INVENTION
CONCERTOS
in 4 and 5 parts
Dedicated
TO THE MOST ILLUSTRIOUS LORD
Lord Wenzel Count von Morzin, Hereditary Lord
of Hohen Elbe, Lomnitz, Tschista, Krzinetz, Kaunitz, Doubek,
and Sowoluska, Current Chamberlain and Counsellor of
His Caesarian and Catholic Majesty
BY DON ANTONIO VIVALDI
Maestro in Italy of the Most Illustrious Aforementioned Lord Count,
Concert Master of the Pio Ospedale della Pietà in Venice,
and Director of Chamber Music to His Most Serene Highness
Prince Philip, Landgrave of Hesse-Darmstadt.
EIGHTH WORK
Book One
AMSTERDAM
At the expense of MICHEL CHARLES LE CÈNE
Bookseller.

No. 520

MOST ILLUSTRIOUS LORD

Thinking to myself of the many years during which I have enjoyed the most signal honour of serving Your Most Illustrious Lordship as Music Master in Italy, I blushed when I reflected that I have not yet given you a demonstration of the profound veneration that I profess towards you; wherefore I resolved to print the present volume in order humbly to present it at the feet of Your Most Illustrious Lordship. Pray do not be surprised if, among these few and feeble concertos, Your Most Illustrious Lordship finds the Four Seasons which have so long enjoyed the indulgence of Your Most Illustrious Lordship's kind generosity, but believe that I have considered it fitting to print them because, while they may be the same, I have added to them, besides the sonnets, a very clear statement of all the things that unfold in them, so that I am sure that they will appear new to you. I will not venture to beseech Your Most Illustrious Lordship to look with a benevolent eye on my weaknesses because I believe that this would be to offend the innate kindness with which Your Most Illustrious Lordship has for so long deigned to show them indulgence. The supreme understanding of music which Your Most Illustrious Lordship possesses and the merit of your most accomplished orchestra will always allow me to live in the certainty that my humble efforts, having reached your most esteemed hands, will enjoy that eminence which they do not deserve. Therefore, nothing remains for me but to beseech Your Most Illustrious Lordship to continue your most generous patronage and never deprive me of the honour of owning myself to be

YOUR MOST ILLUSTRIOUS LORDSHIP'S

Most Humble, Most Devoted,
Most Obliged Servant
ANTONIO VIVALDI

one other work intended for and presumably sent to the count: the bassoon concerto RV 496. Its autograph score, inscribed 'Ma[rchese]: de' Marzin', dates from the early or mid-1720s.[5] Other pieces were evidently sent, both before and after the publication of Op. 8. The count passed on copies of seven Vivaldi concertos to Prince Anton Ulrich von Sachsen-Meiningen in 1723,[6] and records exist, in the Morzin family archive, of payments made to Vivaldi during the period 1724–8.[7]

Another of the composer's titles mentioned on the title-page, *maestro di capella dà camera*, relates to his residence in Mantua from 1718 to 1720 in the service of Prince Philip of Hesse-Darmstadt (1671–1736), from 1714 the Imperial governor of the former independent duchy. Vivaldi's responsibility was for secular music including opera; as we will see, some of the concertos included in Op. 8 appear to have been composed during the period of this appointment. From 1720, he retained his position at Mantua *in absentia*, and continued to cite it on title-pages and other documents until the prince's death. The patronage of Morzin and Prince Philip are just two of many contacts with the Habsburg empire in Vivaldi's career; the next concerto collection that he would publish, Op. 9 in 1727, was dedicated to Charles VI himself, whom he was able to meet in September 1728.[8]

We are thus reminded of the multifarious nature of Vivaldi's activity and the adroitness with which he juggled fresh opportunities, including the chance to publish, as and when they arose. His long association with Venice's Ospedale della Pietà was intermittent, varying in its commitments and of a kind that often permitted him to undertake other work. Recent research has shown that many sacred and instrumental pieces formerly presumed to have been written for that institution were destined for patrons and customers elsewhere, often outside the Venetian state. In the period that concerns us, Vivaldi's most recent position at the Pietà, as *maestro de' concerti* from May 1716, must have lapsed on his appointment to Mantua although he continued to use the title (as Op. 8 shows). He is not known to have acted for the Pietà again until July 1723, when he was contracted – this time as an outsider, not an official *maestro* or teacher – to supply, and (when in Venice) rehearse, two new concertos per month.[9] Under this arrangement, which seems to have lasted until 1735, over 140 concertos were delivered by August 1729.[10] One might naturally expect some of the works written in the early 1720s, whether for that purpose or for other reasons, to appear in Op. 8, for Vivaldi was by no means averse to reusing his pieces. The contents of Op. 8 tell a different story, and very probably have little or no connection with the repertory of the Pietà.

Old and new texts

In his letter of dedication, Vivaldi is at pains to justify the inclusion of *The Four Seasons*, for in reoffering music that Morzin already possessed he risked incurring the patron's displeasure. In mitigation of his impertinence, he alludes to improvements in presentation: '. . . I have added to them, besides the sonnets, a very clear statement of all the things that unfold in them, so that I am sure that they will appear new to you'. This has sometimes been assumed to mean that the sonnets themselves, with their attendant cue-letters that enable cross-reference to particular passages, were added especially for Op. 8, but this is uncertain. Vivaldi's additions were perhaps little more than cosmetic: the quotation of the sonnets' lines at the appropriate points in the music, and various extra explanatory captions that appear here and there. Plate 1 illustrates these features. The only surviving manuscripts of *The Four Seasons* as a set, preserved in Manchester (cited in Table 1, below), show what might be the original system. The sonnets are included with their cue-letters, and the cue-letters appear at their respective locations in the music but without any verbal quotations or other captions: see Plate 2. As an apparatus for cross-reference between sonnet and music, this is uncomplicated and fully functional; the print's captions add little of significance and undermine the purpose of using cue-letters in the first place.

The Manchester manuscripts may be trusted for adjudication on this and other textual points. Although they are non-autograph copies, their particular combination of scribal hands and music-papers leaves little room for doubt that the composer ordered them to be made and that they were copied directly from his own scores, now lost. Seemingly written out in 1726 for presentation in that year to Cardinal Pietro Ottoboni, they postdate the appearance of Op. 8 but accurately transmit a text that is older than the retouched version as published.[11] In stark contrast, the only other extant manuscripts of any of the *Seasons* offer texts either derived from a printed edition (the Paris manuscript of *Spring*, based on the Le Clerc print) or ones that are hopelessly corrupt (the Lund and Genoa copies of *Summer*).[12]

Various clues convince us that the Le Cène edition provides authentic versions of the twelve works, whether revised or not. The nomenclature of the six parts, for instance, follows Vivaldi's own (except that he would rarely mention the cello specifically): *Violino principale* (principal violin), *Violino primo*, *Violino secondo*, *Alto viola* and, in two copies, *Organo e violoncello* (basso continuo and cello, with figured-bass notation).[13] With two bass parts, the print provides all the materials necessary for performance. The intended

Plate 1 *L'estate* (*Summer*, RV 315), first movement, bars 52–120; p. 6 of
the principal violin part of the first edition of Op. 8 (Le Cène, Amsterdam).
London, British Library, g.33.c.

Plate 2   *L'inverno* (*Winter*, RV 297), finale, bars 89–153. Non-autograph
Venetian manuscript: Manchester, Central Library, MS 580 Ct51 (vol. I f. 30r).

ensemble is therefore small, limited to the number of players who can sit or
stand around the non-solo parts as given: neither a medium-sized orchestra
in the late eighteenth-century sense, nor necessarily only one player per part,
although this can work well. The text is largely accurate; its various 'solo' and
'tutti' markings, dynamics, trills and occasional abbreviated notations are
consistent with those that appear regularly throughout Vivaldi's manuscript
scores. It is possible, however, that the figures in the *organo* parts were added,
or at least filled out to become a continuous series, by someone in Amsterdam
– an editorial intervention that a publisher might typically make.[14]
   The edition of Op. 8 published in Paris in 1739 by Le Clerc is in effect not
a distinct source at all; having been based on the Amsterdam print, its musical
text duplicates the readings of Le Cène, including incorrect ones. The

Table 1

Vol.		Title	Key	Identity	Manuscript concordances
I	1:	*La primavera* (*Spring*)	E major	RV 269	Manchester: copy, 5 parts[a] Paris: copy, 5 parts[b]
	2:	*L'estate* (*Summer*)	G minor	RV 315	Manchester: copy, 5 parts[c] Genoa: copy, 5 parts[d] Lund: copy, 5 parts[e]
	3:	*L'autunno* (*Autumn*)	F major	RV 293	Manchester: copy, 5 parts[f]
	4:	*L'inverno* (*Winter*)	F minor	RV 297	Manchester: copy, 5 parts[g]
	5:	*La tempesta di mare* (*The Storm at Sea*)	E♭ major	RV 253	Dresden: autograph, *Organo* part[h] Dresden: copy, 10 parts[i] Manchester: copy, 5 parts[j]
	6:	*Il piacere* (*Pleasure*)	C major	RV 180	none
II	7:		D minor	RV 242[k]	Dresden: autograph, score[l] (first movement only)
	8:		G minor	RV 332[m]	Turin: autograph, score[n]
	9:		D minor	RV 236 (violin) RV 454 (oboe)	Turin: autograph, score[o]
	10:	*La caccia* (*The Hunt*)	B♭ major	RV 362	Turin: autograph, score[p] Dresden: copy, 5 parts[q]
	11:		D major	RV 210	Turin: autograph, score[r] Schwerin: copy, 6 parts[s]
	12:		C major	RV 178 (violin) RV 449 (oboe)	none

Notes to Table 1:
a   *GB-Mp*, MS 580 Ct51 (9).
b   *F-Pn*, D. 8077.
c   *GB-Mp*, MS 580 Ct51 (10).

dedicatory epistle was omitted, naturally enough, but it is curious that only the viola part gives the lines of the *Seasons*' sonnets as captions above the music – a procedure that applies to all the Le Cène parts. It is worth noting here that the delightful obbligato cello part belonging to the slow movement of *Winter* (see Example 25a) became detached and lost from the *organo e violoncello* parts in most extant copies of both editions simply because it was printed on a loose leaf.[15] Consequently, most modern editions, recordings and live performances also lack it.

A grand idea

The content of Op. 8 as a whole, summarized in Table 1, is most perplexing. Whether or not Vivaldi intended it to be enigmatic, its peculiar complexion cries out for explanation – all the more so because of the significance attached to *The Four Seasons* as a notable development in programmatic composition. Purely in terms of Vivaldi's career, Op. 8 represents a significant milestone: his arrival at full maturity as a concerto composer. Music bearing such heavy historical responsibilities deserves to be dated accurately; only then might the set's complexion seem capable of being explained.

The date of publication, 1725, tells us virtually nothing about what Vivaldi did or why and when he did it. We seek instead the date, or dates, when he composed the music and compiled the set, and evidence of his thinking during that period. One naturally presumes that the contents of a publication were finalized by the composer a year or so before the date of issue, allowing for

Notes to Table 1 (*cont.*):

d   *I-Gi(l)*, SS.A.2.10.
e   *S-L*, Wenster, Lit. L, 14.
f   *GB-Mp*, MS 580 Ct51 (11).
g   *GB-Mp*, MS 580 Ct51 (12).
h   *D-Dlb*, Mus. 2389-O-62.
i   *D-Dlb*, Mus. 2389-O-62.
j   *GB-Mp*, MS 580 Ct51 (13).
k   Also published as the first concerto in *Select Harmony . . . XII Concertos . . . Collected from the Works of Antonio Vivaldi . . .* (Walsh & Hare, London, 1730).
l   *D-Dlb*, Mus. 2389-O-44. Autograph inscription: 'fatto p(er) M:° Pisendel'.
m   Also published as the second concerto in *Select Harmony*: see note k.
n   *I-Tn*, Giordano 30, ff. 2–11.
o   *I-Tn*, Foà 32, ff. 41–50. Autograph inscription: 'Con:to p(er) Haubois'.
p   *I-Tn*, Giordano 29, ff. 245–53.
q   *D-Dlb*, Mus. 2389-O-63.
r   *I-Tn*, Giordano 30, ff. 184–206 and Giordano 29, f. 304.
s   *D-SWl*, Mus. 5586.

the time it took for the publisher to receive and process the music. On this basis, and allowing also for some unforeseen delays in the route to press, one might conservatively estimate that Vivaldi defined the collection and despatched its exemplar to Amsterdam in 1724 or 1723. To refine the date further, one looks to the method and nature of the compilation itself. Did Vivaldi compose much of the music especially for Op. 8? Or did he simply select existing compositions? Evidence of the works' approximate composition-dates, besides Vivaldi's own admission that *The Four Seasons* had existed for some time, leaves us in no doubt that the latter procedure applied either totally or in large measure; other collections show this to be the composer's customary method. Op. 8 therefore cannot be regarded as anything other than an anthology; to see in it the kind of collective integrity or musical unity that one might expect of, say, a nineteenth-century song-cycle is to indulge in wishful thinking.

Op. 8 is nevertheless a special case. Lacking the typical features of a made-up anthology, it shows evidence of a new way of thinking on Vivaldi's part. When compiling a set out of works of distinct origins, the best that a composer can do is to match examples that complement each other in some way, or to sort works into sequence according to a musical criterion – their tonic keys, for instance – so that a virtue is made of diversity. Vivaldi's Op. 3, *L'estro armonico* (1711), shows an imaginative arrangement by both key and scoring that was novel for its time. Op. 8 is less consistently organized in that the concertos from No. 5 onwards lack an evident pattern, but its disposition is an advance on those of earlier Vivaldi collections, and innovatory in relation to all eighteenth-century collections until then. The impression created by the high incidence of concertos with special titles is that the process of mixing and matching had intellectual appeal as its basis; the result is a compilation with at least some *implied* collective integrity. Because Vivaldi apparently indulged in cerebral – as opposed to musical – logic, one cannot assume, as one might for other anthologies, that he selected only very recent compositions that would show the world the latest, most progressive state of his art. Some works in Op. 8 were doubtless picked for that reason, but several could not have been. *The Storm at Sea*, for instance, dates back probably to 1716–17 and was surely included as No. 5 not for its modernity but for its value as a good companion to *The Four Seasons*.

The weakness in Vivaldi's scheme is obvious in the difference between the two volumes. Whatever idea he presumably had for presenting unrelated works as the facets of a single concept was not carried through. The first volume has a clear semblance of unity forged by an exclusive use of characterized concertos: taking his cue from *The Four Seasons*, Vivaldi added *The Storm at Sea* and *Pleasure*. The hint of the same general concept within volume II is far less convincing. *The Hunt*, placed in a seemingly insignificant position as No. 10, was perhaps no more selected as a special case than any of the volume's other five works. Did Vivaldi abandon his idea halfway through the project and resort to picking works indiscriminately? Or could it be that, although he would have preferred to maintain a consistent approach, he simply had no other concertos with special titles to draw upon at that time?

We look to the title of the collection for enlightenment, admittedly without great confidence. Vivaldi's names for other concerto collections – *L'estro armonico* ('Harmonic Inspiration' or 'Harmonic Whim', Op. 3, 1711); *La stravaganza* ('Extravagance', Op. 4, *c*. 1714); *La cetra* ('The Cither', Op. 9, 1727) – are striking and memorable, but they are far from meaningful in relation to the music. The composer's motive in selecting them is surely one born not of pretentiousness but of an intuitive feel for successful marketing. In the competitive world of concerto publishing a set with a name stood a greater chance of attracting attention than one advertised simply as 'Concerti'; a title full of tantalizing promise had the additional advantage of implying that the music was extraordinary and well worth buying and playing. Vivaldi's policy should not be dismissed as merely a commercial ploy, however. He deserves credit for understanding, more than his rivals did, that concertos needed to find a new and attractive identity as multi-purpose repertory for concerts of all kinds, public or private, now that they had shed their former courtly and sacred functions. There is probably no better explanation than this for Vivaldi's experiments in the genre over many years, and in Op. 8 we see not only some of the fruits of his search for methods but also, perhaps, his uncertainty about the way forward.

'Il cimento dell'armonia e dell'inventione' is a more meaningful title than the others in that it apparently alludes to a compositional approach. Whether or not the allusion has substance in relation to the music is more difficult to judge, for the wording still smacks of 'handy label' as well as 'artistic theme'. 'Harmony' is, to the eighteenth-century mind, the traditional craft of composition: a rational, acquired art. 'Invention' is the un-learnt human imagination with which 'harmony' can be transformed. Vivaldi had evidently latched on to a real distinction between the two concepts that is certainly in evidence in Op. 8. But much depends on the meaning of 'Il cimento'. One might be tempted to translate it rather too freely as 'the contest', as if two creative forces, *Harmony* and *Invention* in allegorical personification, are at war with each other for supremacy in music. It is most doubtful that Vivaldi intended such a dramatic vision or meant that harmony and invention oppose and ultimately exclude each other. More accurately, 'il cimento' equates to the English word 'assay': a test or trial for quality – in this case a test of both harmony and invention, which are complementary and can coexist. On balance, then, we might acknowledge three things about the title and why Vivaldi chose it. First, there is some substance to it as a reflection of his thinking. Second, it served as good publicity by implying that his music passes the test. Third, it is perhaps an afterthought nevertheless, possibly chosen to justify the selection of both characterized and non-characterized concertos when the former type is preferred and to disguise whatever failure the composer sensed was implicit in that compromised selection.

An abundance or a dearth of titles?

The validity of the last argument hinges on whether or not Vivaldi had other concertos with special titles at his disposal. If some were available, why did he not package them into the second volume of Op. 8? This is puzzling because we now know that he was preoccupied with writing characterized concertos – and with grouping them in sets, too – before and during the time when Op. 8 might be presumed, on the basis of the date of publication alone, to have been assembled.

The period of that preoccupation begins in the mid-1710s, peaks early in the 1720s and peters out by the 1730s. *The Storm at Sea* (RV 253, the version published in Op. 8),[16] *Il ritiro* ('Retiring', RV 294a, published in 1716 or 1717 as Op. 7 No. 10) and 'The Cuckow' (RV 335, first published in 1717)[17] are probably the earliest surviving examples. *The Four Seasons* are likely to be of the same mid-1710s' vintage. The autograph manuscript of *La caccia* (*The Hunt*) has been dated to *c.* 1718–20.[18] The next datable group is assigned to the year 1720, and for this there is real evidence of a devotion on Vivaldi's part to the notion of a conceptually related set of violin concertos: *Il sospetto* ('Suspicion', RV 199), *L'inquietudine* ('Anxiety', RV 234) and *Il riposo* ('Rest', RV 270), whose autograph draft scores share precisely the same variety of music-paper and some special markings, were seemingly designed as companion works.[19] In the early and mid-1720s came several others – not all solo violin concertos and without necessarily any conceptual links between them: *Il gardellino* ('The Goldfinch', RV 90); *La pastorella* ('The Shepherd-ess', RV 95); *La notte* ('Night', RV 104); *Concerto madrigalesco* (RV 129); *Concerto alla rustica* ('Rustic Concerto', RV 151); *L'amoroso* ('Amorousness',

RV 271); a changed version of *Il ritiro* (RV 294); *Il Proteo ossia il mondo al rovescio* ('Proteus, or The World Upside-Down', RV 544 and RV 572) and *Concerto funebre* ('Funereal Concerto', RV 579).[20] To the early 1720s belongs also an aborted plan to write a concerto called *La disunione* ('Disunion').[21] By the late 1720s, Vivaldi's interest in titles had largely evaporated. Some ambivalence is evident: RV 277, left untitled in a manuscript collection dated 1728, resurfaced in 1729 as *Il favorito* ('The Favourite', Op. 11 No. 2). Of extant works, all that remain are two whose titles allude to the music's imitation of instruments: *Conca* ('The Conch', RV 163), almost certainly composed in *c.* 1730 during the composer's visit to Bohemia,[22] and *Il corneto di posta* ('The Post-Horn', RV 363) which has yet to be dated.

A concentration of eight titled works – *Il Proteo* (RV 572), *Il ritiro* (RV 294), *Il riposo*, *L'inquietudine*, *Il gardellino* (RV 90), *La tempesta di mare* (RV 253), *La pastorella* and *L'ottavina* – among the twelve concerto manuscripts given by Vivaldi to the musicians of Ottoboni's court demonstrates the composer's inclination, in around 1723–4, to 'market' his special wares in combination with each other.[23] Finally, our review would not be complete without mention of four flute concertos with geographical titles – *La Francia*, *La Spagna*, *L'Inghilterra* and *Il Gran Mogul* (France, Spain, England and India) – that, sadly, are lost and therefore undatable, but whose names alone show again that Vivaldi was inclined to fashion sets according to extra-musical criteria.[24]

The focal date

Op. 8 samples only relatively early concertos with titles: the cut-off point lies around 1718–20. We are thus led to suspect that the time when Op. 8 was compiled was no later than *c.* 1720: at least five years before the collection was published. If the degree to which Vivaldi used concertos with titles were the only evidence, such a startling conclusion would seem beyond belief. We need to be reasonably confident that the assumption on which that conclusion is based – that Vivaldi would have included more titled concertos if more had existed at the time – is correct. The collection's title, after all, leaves open the possibility that he positively favoured the mixture of works as it stands rather than merely settled for it.

The identity of the collection's works *without* titles dispels those uncertainties because it supports exactly the same conclusion for dating. Vivaldi's own stock of manuscripts, preserved in Turin, is particularly rich in concertos composed in the early and mid-1720s; many must be examples provided for the Pietà from July 1723. From this substantial repertory he did not draw any work for Op. 8, titled or untitled, but would surely have done so if he had constructed the collection at a time close to 1725. The correlations that do exist between Op. 8 and Vivaldi's manuscripts point with fascinating clarity to a distinctly earlier date of assembly. The loss of autograph materials for certain works regrettably means that the picture will remain incomplete; it is particularly unfortunate that, in the absence of clues from manuscripts, RV 180 and RV 178/449 cannot be located in a chronological scheme. Discounting the special case of *The Four Seasons*, already considered, let us review the evidence work by work.

RV 253, La tempesta di mare ('The Storm at Sea' = *Op. 8 No. 5)*

The parts preserved in Dresden are of Venetian provenance;[25] those in the hands of the violinist Johann Georg Pisendel and another person, as well as the sole autograph part, were almost certainly written out when Pisendel and his companions from the Saxon court visited Venice in 1716–17. The Manchester source also emanates directly from Vivaldi's own activities,[26] and belongs to the group of manuscripts given to Ottoboni, mentioned earlier, although the parts for *La tempesta di mare* were not written out for that purpose. The second violin part, in fact, was notated on music-paper that has been assigned to the Mantuan period *c.* 1718–20 – exactly the same variety that was employed for the autograph scores of RV 210, 332 and 362, concordant with Op. 8 Nos. 11, 8 and 10 respectively.[27] Significant differences between the three surviving texts (Dresden, Manchester, Le Cène) suggest, moreover, that the version recorded in Op. 8 is *earlier* than that of the Manchester parts.[28] It is impossible to be certain about this in the absence of an autograph score that would show the exact nature of textual revisions, but here we have the slightest of hints that Vivaldi began to compile Op. 8 a little before the time, *c.* 1720, that we have estimated so far.

RV 242 (= Op. 8 No. 7)

The Dresden autograph draft, containing only the first movement, was almost certainly given to Pisendel (to whom it is inscribed) during his visit to Venice and studies with Vivaldi in 1716–17.[29] Although the corresponding movement of Op. 8 No. 7 is a quite different version, we may be reasonably sure that the work existed in some form before *c.* 1720. Vivaldi may have redrafted the music especially for Op. 8.

RV 332 (= Op. 8 No. 8)

The Turin autograph draft is believed to date from *c*. 1718–20, like those of
RV 210 and RV 362 (*La caccia*) and one of the Manchester parts for RV 253.
The texts of the autograph and the print correspond very closely; the
manuscript's few textual alterations were perhaps made in connection with
Op. 8.

RV 236/454 (= Op. 8 No. 9)

The Turin autograph draft appears to have been created in or very near to
1720: Vivaldi used the same variety of music-paper for his manuscript of the
opera *La verità in cimento* RV 739, first performed in Venice in the autumn
of that year.[30] RV 236/454 might indeed be the last of the works in Op. 8 to
have been composed. Textual clues leave little room for doubt that the version
sent to Amsterdam was copied directly from the Turin score. The solo part's
quaver f^1 in bar 72 of the first movement, for instance, is an error in No. 9
(reproduced in the Ricordi edition too) that stems from the fact that Vivaldi's
notehead in the autograph, for the correct pitch $g\sharp^1$, is poorly drawn. Some
alterations bear witness to Vivaldi's decision to publish the piece as a violin
concerto (the version known today as RV 236). His inscription at the head of
the manuscript shows that the work began life as an oboe concerto (RV 454);
in bars 91–101 of the first movement, however, the original solo part is deleted
and replaced by a revised passage together with the words 'Viol:º Principale'
– both the notes and the solo instrument intended for Op. 8.

RV 362, La caccia ('The Hunt' = Op. 8 No. 10)

The Turin autograph draft is believed to date from *c*. 1718–20, like those of
RV 210 and RV 332 and one of the Manchester parts for RV 253. It shows
several alterations to the text. Op. 8 duplicates the revised readings but this
does not necessarily mean that the changes were made when Vivaldi compiled
the set; they might date from the drafting of the work in the first instance.
Some significant variants show, however, that further revision of the work
occurred in a way that is not evident from the Turin score. Some changes
might have been written directly into the exemplar sent to Amsterdam: bar
112/283 of the finale as given in the print, for example, does not exist in the
Turin and Dresden manuscripts. Others are more likely to have been notated
by Vivaldi in a further manuscript score, now lost. Most interesting of all is

Plate 3 *La caccia* (*The Hunt*, RV 362), first movement, bars 1–25.
Autograph: Turin, Biblioteca Nazionale Universitaria, Giordano 29, f. 245r.

his apparent decision to simplify the viola and bass parts' drum-rhythm in the first movement (bars 1–18, 64–9 and 112–17): in the Turin score the first beat in each bar is consistently given as a quaver followed by two semiquavers (see Plate 3). The Dresden copy, a set of parts of German provenance,[31] records the two-quaver rhythm known also from the print, but in other respects (besides some minor variants in a harpsichord part) follows the Turin version.

RV 210 (= Op. 8 No. 11)

The Turin autograph draft is believed to date from *c*. 1718–20, like those of RV 332 and 362 and one of the Manchester parts for RV 253. This dating is valid for the score of RV 210 only in its original state. Vivaldi later made two sets of revisions to the fast movements: first some fairly minor changes,[32] and then substantial ones, physical as well as textual, using leaves of varieties of paper that appear to date from the early to mid-1720s. Apart from the last three bars of the finale, Op. 8 No. 11 duplicates the original version, showing none of the results of the autograph's transformation.

To summarize: It would appear that Vivaldi assembled the set in or a little before 1720, revising some of the music in the process. For volume II, he faced a problem: he could not fill it with concertos with titles because no further unpublished examples existed – except, perhaps, *The Hunt*. His only options were to compose some new ones, or to use untitled works. In the event, he followed the latter course; some of the works selected, notably RV 210 in its original state, RV 236/454, RV 332 and RV 362, were very recent or brand new compositions.

But let us suppose that Vivaldi at least attempted to write further works on allusive themes with a view to including them in the second volume, before opting for the untitled ones. It is conceivable that RV 362 (*The Hunt*) did not yet exist and was composed and given its title precisely for this reason (see p. 52). We might further conjecture that Vivaldi pursued his plan to the extent of composing *Il sospetto*, *L'inquietudine* and *Il riposo*, which, as we have seen, have a putative date of 1720 and may well have been designed in quick succession as a trilogy or parts of a larger set. Their allusive themes certainly complement that of *The Hunt* sufficiently to be considered as good companions – better, indeed, than those of most of the other titled concertos. It may not be purely coincidental, either, that the single variety of music-paper on which Vivaldi drafted them is the very same type as that of the autograph of RV 236/454 – the oboe concerto that he adopted, or perhaps reluctantly settled for, as Op. 8 No. 9. We cannot know the order in which these four scores were created, but we can at least surmise that they are approximately coeval.[33] Vivaldi's two actions in question – the composition of *Il sospetto*, *L'inquietudine* and *Il riposo*, and the selection of works for volume II in the scheme that Op. 8 preserves – took place at times close enough for us to suspect that they were in some way related. If they were, one wonders how and why the former led to the latter, and why *The Hunt* managed to survive in volume II when no other titled concerto did.

Another difficult question remains. Why did it take roughly five years for the assembled collection to be published? It is surely probable that Vivaldi sent the set's exemplar to Amsterdam promptly in *c.* 1720. If for some reason he had delayed the project until a time closer to 1725, this would be reflected in a choice of more modern music for volume II. On the contrary, the contents of Op. 8 hint that Vivaldi's aspirations for the set were compromised by a need to expedite the despatch with considerable urgency. The inordinate delay is much more likely to have been caused in Amsterdam.

In 1720, the publishing house was owned by Estienne Roger but run by his daughter and successor Jeanne. Michel-Charles Le Cène, having married Jeanne's elder sister Françoise, succeeded as head of the firm in 1722 after the deaths in that year of both Estienne and Jeanne. Vivaldi may well have become disenchanted with the manner in which Opp. 5–7 were issued in quick succession in *c.* 1716–17 under Jeanne's imprint; some of the texts are faulty, certain works in Op. 7 are probably spurious, and all three publications, lacking dedications, were most likely brought out on the publisher's initiative without Vivaldi's express permission. However, our surmised dating for the assembly and despatch of Op. 8 rules out the theory, recently advanced, that the long interval between the publication dates of Op. 7 and Op. 8 indicates that Vivaldi actually boycotted the firm.[34] Whatever grievance he felt did not stop him from planning Op. 8 and making it available – whether on request from Amsterdam or by proffering it. A lack of cooperation might have come instead from Jeanne Roger and her father if the composer had seemed to them to protest too much; perhaps they ignored the set after receiving it, unwilling to finance its printing. With Le Cène came eventual *rapprochement*, as the appearance in rapid succession of Opp. 9–12 in 1727–9 attests. But although Le Cène looked with favour on Op. 8 and (according to the title-page) financed its printing, he did not do so immediately on taking over the business in 1722. There is good reason, indeed, to suppose that by November 1724 Vivaldi had grown tired of waiting and had come to believe that Op. 8 would never appear. What else, other than a resolve to act independently of Amsterdam, could have caused him to seek financial support for a limited edition of twenty-four concertos to be sold by subscription?[35] Wind of that initiative might have spurred Le Cène into action.

The letter of dedication was probably written only at that late stage – in 1725 – when finally Vivaldi could be certain that Op. 8 was in the press.[36] Its apologetic tone attests to the composer's embarrassment over the long delay. Doubtless he was also disappointed that *The Four Seasons*, once so fresh, reached the public as old music.

Ritornello forms

Op. 8 exemplifies a state of fast-movement design that had matured greatly by 1720. Largely on the strengths of Opp. 3 and 4, an earlier variety of Vivaldian ritornello form had influenced European composition on a wide scale well before the present works were written. Quantz attests that he used Vivaldi's concertos, with their 'magnificent ritornellos', as models from 1714 onwards;[1] by the late 1710s, J. S. Bach had long since absorbed Vivaldian principles into his style and was making distinct innovations. Vivaldi's own advances discernible in Op. 8 are therefore a development parallel to a great deal of ritornello-form composition elsewhere, not the root cause of it. Op. 8 helped, rather, to generate a second wave of influence, particularly in France and among a new generation of Italian composers. Echoes of Op. 8 are heard, for instance, in Pietro Locatelli's concertos and *introduttioni teatrali* of the early 1730s. Meanwhile, Vivaldi's approach had continued to move on: his implementations of ritornello form are not nearly as entrenched in one particular method as might be imagined.

We concentrate, below, on the fast movements of Op. 8 Nos. 5–12, reserving discussion of *The Four Seasons* mostly for Chapter 6. The object, here and in Chapters 4 and 5 too, is to examine Vivaldi's *modus operandi* of *c*. 1716–20 for concertos that are not programmatic, so that we are equipped to distinguish between what is reasonably 'normal' and what is unique in the *Seasons*.

The initial ritornello

For Vivaldi, the first ritornello is the movement's essence: a zest to be encapsulated immediately, irrespective of what happens afterwards. It is not merely thematic material, and does not have to be energetic. Example 1 quotes from contrasting cases, illustrating how the head-motif alone instantly determines the piece's character on all immediate planes: melodic, rhythmic, harmonic and tonal. As an appealing sound-world particularly affected by the

Example 1   Head-motifs: (a) No. 6, I; (b) No. 7, I

choice of key, the whole ritornello impresses itself so strongly that the listener not only anticipates its recurrence but actually desires it. In Op. 8 we see Vivaldi reaping the tactical rewards: the power to meet or just as easily deny the listener's expectation, and the freedom to offer solo episodes that work even when their contents bear little relation to the rest of the music.

After an opening ritornello of such dynamism, the nose-heavy movement will plummet unless interest and momentum are maintained. Vivaldi sometimes fails to satisfy; the first Allegro of Op. 3 No. 2 in G minor begins with an incandescence that fizzles out towards the end. But by the time of Op. 8 he had learned to manipulate the recurrences of the ritornello and the timing of tonal change in a more telling way. Most importantly, he had developed a strategy for solo episodes that keeps the movement in full flight: the ritornellos can safely diminish in effect if the episodes increase in their intensity. A cadenza or cadenza-like passage is regularly included in the final episode not simply to provide the soloist with an expressive moment; it is a climax of structural significance. The natural tension between *tutti* and solo periods is greatly increased by the fact that their respective purposes do not coincide and are essentially contradictory. This is perhaps Vivaldi's greatest contribution to the concertante principle, proving false any suspicion that his solo concertos are simply vehicles for extravagant display.

Most initial ritornellos in Op. 8 conform to the textbook type with at least three parts or 'elements', but are rarely as simple as this sounds. The opening of No. 6 (*Pleasure*) provides a fairly straightforward example. The first element, the excursive 'antecedent' (A), progresses emphatically to the dominant chord – Example 1a – and is then extended to bar 8, reaching dominant harmony again. The process of extension, or *Fortspinnung* ('spin-ning-out'), is continued with the second element, a sequential 'consequent' (B, bars 9–13), and concluded with a short cadential element (C, bars 14–15).

We may describe this ritornello as 'mono-figurative'. Common to all three elements are the patterned quavers in the bass and the violins' syncopation reminiscent of the second element of *Spring*; it is the combination of the two, at the appropriate tempo, that produces a principal Vivaldian hallmark: rhythmic drive. The ritornello's sound-world may reflect the 'pleasure' of the work's title (though its general character is common among Vivaldi's concertos): bright, positive and essentially agreeable in mood. Compare this with other common-time ritornellos designed to be taken at a similar pace and we find both close relationships and marked contrasts. That of the first movement of *Spring* has a greater brightness that comes from string-playing in E major, and heaviness from a bass proceeding largely in crotchets. The first ritornello of No. 7 (Example 1b quotes its opening) conveys an utterly different sense even though its construction is basically similar (ABC^{1}C^2) to that of No. 6. Its mildly depressed, introspective quality – something that Vivaldi found hard to resist when writing in D minor – comes mainly from diminished and augmented intervals between violins and bass and the lethargy of the tied notes.

Vivaldi's ritornellos, including cases like this with some counterpoint, are homophonically conceived with an impetus governed by immensely strong cadential forces. Having become familiar with his style, it is difficult for us to appreciate just how stunningly original it is in this respect. No other composer of his generation had the audacity, or foresight, to articulate harmony as slowly as in the first movement of *L'inquietudine* RV 234 (roughly contemporary, as we saw in Chapter 2, with the most modern works in Op. 8), where each chord persists for three or four bars of 12/8 metre in a ritornello almost devoid of melody. The ritornello that opens No. 9 demonstrates particularly clearly a kind of magnetic attraction between tonic and dominant poles when harmonic rhythm is slow. We sense that each move to dominant or tonic is a shift as essential to further advance as the shift of weight from one leg to the other is to walking. But having mastered walking, Vivaldi had learnt to vary his step and to skip. So true is his structural harmonic logic that it enabled him to use melody bereft of lyricism and adopt considerable irregularities in phrasing. Who else could have passed off the seven-bar antecedent of No. 9 (Example 2) so naturally? The phrase has tripartite

Example 2   No. 9, I, bars 1–9

melody (bars 1–2, 3–4 and 5–7) and bipartite harmony (tonic–dominant twice, bars 1–4 and 5–7). To be regular, it would need an eighth bar to form a pair of dominant bars with bar 7, but further rest would dislocate the violin parts. Bar 7 alone has sufficient force to attract the consequent.

We begin to see how easily Vivaldi butts elements together in a modular method. To be compatible with each other, they do not necessarily have to share thematic motifs; they need only to have complementary dominant and tonic poles. One that ends on the dominant will normally attract another that begins on the tonic; progress is further advanced if the tonic chord is altered, as in bar 8 of No. 9, to create instant harmonic digression. Some refreshing tonic-to-tonic joins are to be found: in the initial ritornello of No. 6, for instance, where the end of the consequent meets the cadence (bars 13–14).

Tonic-ending phrases are more frequently interlocked with the beginning of the next element. Anacrusic phrases tend to dovetail naturally, as the opening ritornello of No. 7 shows. When anacrusis is not involved, interlocking produces an urgency in the music as the flow of elements is telescoped. This effect may be heard in the ritornello of the finale of No. 7: a classic mono-figurative construction in the form ABC, shown schematically in Example 3a. The antecedent may initially sound like a simple four-bar phrase with harmony descending to the dominant, but its five-bar melody is designed to lead on to the tonic chord in bar 5 and thus to dovetail with the consequent.

In this instance Vivaldi does not allow the harmonic logic of the sequence to run its full course, suspending it at bar 11 on the dominant. The result, despite prolongation of dominant harmony through four further bars, is a

Example 3   Comparison of sequences

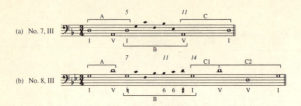

telescoped ritornello shorter than many others in a rapid 3/4 metre. In the case of the ritornello of the finale of No. 8 (Example 3b), the sequence is broken, from bar 11, with a perfect-cadential progression that pre-empts the function that would otherwise apply next. Thus a need is created for further spinning-out, with a new excursive phrase (C^1, from bar 14) that shifts the weight back to the dominant at bar 18. Even this is not enough to undo the suppressive effect of the altered sequence, and yet more music addressed to the dominant (C^2, from bar 18) is required to create sufficient anticipation of the period's conclusion.

A sequential consequent, although clearly a favourite device, is not always present; the ritornello that opens *Spring* demonstrates how repetition of initial and cadential phrases can compensate for the absence of a 'normal' consequent. The ritornello of the finale of No. 10 (*The Hunt*) is similar; its brief four-bar phrase in the tonic minor key (bars 13–16) is more an interlude between the antecedent and the repeated cadential phrase than an actual consequent.[2] Here is a rare case of a dominant ending butted against a dominant continuation (bars 12 and 13), and the effect is to suspend the flow of the music rather than force it on. After an antecedent that so stubbornly adheres to the tonic, a passage of complementary hiatus on the dominant is all that is required.

The finale of No. 12 possesses a sequential consequent (bars 11–18/116–23) that is far from routine. With a harmonic rhythm slower than usual, its expansiveness is a necessary compensation for the lack of excursive progress beforehand. The antecedent, not unlike the opening of Monteverdi's *Beatus vir (primo)* published in 1640, is a curious six-fold repetition of a one-bar unit; its perfect-cadential effect needs somehow to be undone. Another special consequent is found in the first movement of No. 8: a sequence that ascends from Bb major to C minor and then to D minor. Outside *The Four Seasons*, this is the only movement in the collection to begin with a tonally 'open'

Example 4   No. 9, III (a) bars 1–2; (b) bars 10–11

period: a somewhat old-fashioned phenomenon. A product of the key-change is the interesting parallel between the melodies of the antecedent and the cadential element from the end of bar 9, where the motif first heard in bar 1 is given a fresh harmonization.

It is not uncommon, indeed, for Vivaldi to use the cadential element imaginatively as the means of crowning what has gone before while fusing the ritornello as a rounded design. An 'ABC' ritornello construction naturally invites this approach since a regressive 'C' can be a cadential mirror-image of the excursive 'A'; the moody ritornello that opens the violin concerto in C minor *Il sospetto* (RV 199) is a perfect example. Perhaps the best case in Op. 8 occurs in the finale of No. 9, where the cadential element from bar 8/146 has several important functions and features. It is based on and incorporates the antecedent and is therefore very much its skewed reflection. Rather like the playing of a trump card, it interrupts and drastically curtails the consequent before the sequence can reach the dominant, and then interrupts its own progress by restarting in bar 9. These effects rhyme with the ritornello's curious opening on a 6–3 chord (Example 4a), where the crotchet b♭^{1} is best regarded as an appoggiatura: it is as if the beginning of the movement itself is an interruption. The cadential element puts a subtle gloss on that appoggiatura motif by converting the crotchets to a principal note followed by a long anticipatory note (f ^{1}–e^1, bars 10 and 11): Example 4b.

Cadential elements in Op. 8 differ greatly, partly because their function and extent are influenced by the treatment of the elements that precede them, as we have seen. They can be abrupt, prolonged, delayed, repeated or paired with another cadential phrase. The ten-bar example in the finale of No. 6, from the anacrusis to bar 16/120, functions as a counterbalance to the antecedent–consequent pair. By curtailing the consequent (bars 8–15) with an imperfect cadence, Vivaldi set up the possibility of repeating in bars 15–19 the music of bars 1–4, and thus overtly turned the ritornello into a binary construction. It is an approach ideal for the context. Possessing the flavour of a Haydnesque

Example 5   No. 10 (*The Hunt*), I, bars 1–19

rondo, this quirky *buffo* theme in 2/4 metre – certainly to be taken at a faster pace than Vivaldi's allegro movements notated in common time – thoroughly deserves its many internal repetitions.

Vivaldi occasionally employs a markedly effusive 'grand' cadence. One case, bars 12–15 of No. 5, tantalizingly presents a standard progression in slow motion like the one that heralds the entry of the voices in Handel's *Zadok the Priest*. Another is the cadence (plus its *piano* reprise) of the first movement of No. 12: bars 14–20. Relating back to the soloist's semiquavers in the 'premature' cadential progression of bars 9–11, it releases tension wound up by the motto-like return to the dominant (bars 11–14). As it rises to the high tonic, the music is crowned with the 'touch of the subdominant' (bars 15–16 and 18) – much as in the initial ritornello of Bach's first Brandenburg concerto.

The ritornellos of both movements of No. 11, containing fugal antecedents, last twice as long as the telescoped examples that begin the finales of Nos. 7 and 9. Their fugal expositions, each ending on the tonic, neither provoke nor easily permit extension – especially when further four-part counterpoint is shunned. In the finale, Vivaldi resorts to a quick fix in the harmony at bar 17/176 to make possible the ensuing sequence.[3] The ritornello of the first movement emerges from the rut of tonic-orientated harmony only at bar 21, after several phrases of spinning-out including (at bars 9–12) an antiphonal passage in the *stile tromba*.[4]

In contrast, the thirty-one-bar ritornello of the first movement of No. 10 (*The Hunt*) is neither long-winded nor incoherent; paradoxically, it is more economical than many others of fewer bars. By contracting the antecedent–consequent formula while inflating the harmonic rhythm, Vivaldi has accommodated imitative upper parts that dovetail in a novel way. Example 5 shows bars 1–19 in reduction (see also Plate 3). The second violins chase the firsts – but at three bars' remove. Against each pair of chords, the violins play in turn a four-bar motif and a compensating two-bar scalar tag (beamed as *x* and y, respectively). The whole phrase, tripartite in six-bar harmonic units (as beamed on the lower staff), condenses the functions of antecedent and consequent into one.

The framework

By the mid-1710s Vivaldi had formulated one of the fundamental principles of his brand of ritornello form: that a movement's second and subsequent ritornellos are rarely identical to the first. Only one of the eleven ritornello-form fast movements in Op. 6 (the first of No. 6, RV 239) possesses a central or final *tutti* period that duplicates the initial ritornello. Nowhere is this procedure to be found in Op. 8. As one writer has put it, 'Vivaldi is a deviant Vivaldian' because he allows a ritornello to recur in its original form far less frequently than the composers who aped his method.[5] He had realized that the predictability inherent in the alternation of solo and *tutti* periods, which could so easily debilitate a movement, can be harnessed as a positive force for musical development provided that listeners' expectations are manipulated. To that end, initial ritornellos must be of the right type. They are modular so that they may be broken apart; they are lengthy so that they may be shortened. Op. 8 shows too that Vivaldi employs certain gambits for the early central ritornellos and quite different ones for the closing ones. These tactics are intrinsically linked to tonal strategy, discussed later in this chapter.

A second *tutti* period such as bars 29–35 in the first movement of No. 6 (*Pleasure*) is a complete ritornello fulfilling the allied functions of segregating solo episodes and affirming the new key; and yet the differences between it and the initial ritornello are significant. Shorn of most of the original period's *Fortspinnung*, it concludes with a surprising abruptness that precipitates the next episode. It retains enough of the original music to guarantee its familiarity while destroying a little of the theme's predictability. This is a common type of second ritornello in Op. 8, where elements A and C are butted against each other. In the first movement of No. 10 (*The Hunt*), the collision in bars 69–70 of incompatible elements produces an unusually strong aural jolt. The same arrangement of pruned antecedent and cadential element is sometimes employed for more than one central *tutti* period; in this way a movement's tonal steps acquire a noticeable pattern. The third and fourth ritornellos in the finale of No. 9 (bars 33–9/171–7 and 52–7/190–5) are not exactly similar, however. Because the latter lacks the fourth bar of the head-motif, the resulting tonic–tonic join in the middle of bar 55/193 increases the degree of abruptness beyond that of the previous ritornello.

A feature common in earlier concertos that hardly ever appears in Op. 8 is a *tutti* period in the first half or two-thirds of a movement that consists only of the antecedent. Unlike the A+C construction that has a full close, it is a 'partial ritornello': a throw-back to the 'motto' as used by Torelli and Albinoni – and by Vivaldi himself in his concertos without soloist. Its rarity in Op. 8 suggests that by the late 1710s, if not earlier, Vivaldi was intent upon a complete separation between early *tutti* and solo periods not only by means of thematic differentiation and tonal progression but also by avoiding phrase connection. He employs element A by itself only when the music demands its 'kick-start' effect: it invites an episode that grows out of or answers it, rather than one that initiates a new event. An example is the second *tutti* period, bars 22–5/160–3, of the finale of No. 9. Its presence here relates to the avoidance of modulation in the preceding episode; the head-motif alone is enough to provoke the solo that will produce the first tonal step, by now overdue. The tactic resembles that of the operatic aria's *Devise*,[6] employed in Vivaldi's Op. 3 and with great frequency in the oboe concertos of Albinoni.

The norm in Op. 8 is for an early central ritornello to be closed by a perfect cadence, whether this is the original cadential material (abbreviated or adapted) or an all-purpose tag of the kind found in many of Vivaldi's works: No. 11, I, bars 56–7, for instance. Elements that were not originally adjacent sometimes require special treatment; bar 38/143 in the finale of No. 12 is the glue with which the tonic-ending antecedent is bonded to the dominant-beginning cadential element.

The presence of the antecedent and absence of the consequent are important clues to the composer's thinking. Common sense dictates that a *tutti* period might not sound like a ritornello unless it begins with the head-motif, and that the consequent can be dispensed with if the object is to create a brief central ritornello closed by a cadence. But there is surely more to Vivaldi's method than short-term expediency. As a means of orientating the listener throughout the whole movement, the antecedent is almost always retained for ritornellos that mark each excursive step in the tonal scheme; it is frequently absent from final periods when further steps will not occur. The consequent, too, is used for aural cross-reference between one part of the movement and another – but usually between points at greater remove than successive ritornellos. In the first movement of No. 6, for instance, the sequence of bars 9–13 recurs only once at the end of the piece (bars 77–81), without the antecedent; the same is true of the concerto's finale.

The withholding of the consequent until the tonic key has been restored is one of Vivaldi's most effective ways of overriding the multi-step pattern of *tutti*–solo alternation so that the listener gains a sense of the whole conception. It is significant, too, that most of the consequents in Op. 8 are sequential. Some commentators have dismissed the composer's fondness for sequence as a weakness betraying a paucity of other methods of extension. But if this alleged weakness exists anywhere in Op. 8, it is confined to solo episodes. Sequential consequents are not merely useful extensions; they are the passages that many listeners will find the most attractive and piquant, and Vivaldi well understood how to tap their potency as a force to be tantalizingly withheld and finally unleashed. Much of the power of the first movement of No. 9 must be attributed to the sudden arrival of the unprefaced consequent in bar 79 immediately after the return to the tonic key – and not a little to the inspired alliance of rhythm and harmony in the sequence itself. A second wham follows in bar 109. In the finale of the same concerto, the return of the consequent (bar 68/206) produces its 'double take' effect and deliciously glosses the soloist's final cadence with a *tierce de Picardie*. The final significance of the consequent in the finale of No. 12 (from bar 84/189) is even prefigured in the previous solo. By requiring the consequent to oust the antecedent in the hierarchy of principal elements, Vivaldi subscribed to a quasi-dramatic notion of struggle and resolution over the course of a movement. It is a game-plan, indeed, that explains much about *The Four Seasons*.

The late return of the consequent is frequently part of a standard 'end-play' consisting of the final three periods: the last solo sandwiched between two *tutti* passages. In its purest form, exemplified well in the first movement of No. 6, the complex occurs after the tonic key has been reached; alternatively, the modulation takes place in the first *tutti* period in the end-play. Largely shunned earlier in a movement, a short, partial ritornello that kick-starts the solo is ideal for the penultimate *tutti*, and is typically the antecedent pruned or drastically curtailed (No. 9, III, bars 64–5/202–3). The final *tutti*, when it consists of the consequent and cadence, will seem in retrospect to complete a ritornello that has been 'dramatically' interrupted by the soloist. The solo itself, freed of the function of key-change, can range from a brief flourish to a substantial written-out cadenza.

Op. 8 alone shows, however, that Vivaldi took alternative approaches; we should not expect his ritornello forms, not even those that are roughly contemporary with each other, to match a universal blueprint any more than we would expect this of, say, Mozart's sonata-form structures. Sometimes the sequential consequent recurs at a much earlier stage, and in the first movements of Nos. 7 and 10 it does not recur at all. In the case of No. 10 (*The Hunt*), we may infer from revisions in the work's autograph manuscript that

Vivaldi could have engineered a repeat of the consequent if he had wanted to.[7] Is the complete withdrawal of the sequence therefore the ultimate extension of the principle of drawing out the listener's expectation? Is the element a dangled carrot that the donkey can never reach? Perhaps not; although Vivaldi is never as guilty as Geminiani, whose sublime consequent in the first Allegro of Op. 3 No. 1 is most frustratingly never heard again, his failure to bring back, seemingly without good reason, some of his best ideas has not gone unnoticed.[8] On the other hand, the phenomenon is a feature of enough movements outside Op. 8 to suggest that it is a symptom not of sloppy composition but of Vivaldi distancing himself from a tactic before it became too conventional.[9] A general impression created by his concertos of the 1720s is that he came to prefer harmonically static ritornellos, loaded with motto themes and multiple cadences, to which sequential lyricism is not ideally suited. The *tutti* periods in both fast movements of *The Hunt* reflect this trend more than most in Op. 8.

Vivaldi shows a passing concern to end a whole work in a special way by adding to or otherwise varying the last ritornello of the finale. Such adjustments range from the simple extra cadence in the last bar of No. 9 to the thirty-bar extension of the final period in *The Storm at Sea*. No. 10 ends with a unison cadence of a decidedly pre-Classical flavour. The closing passage in No. 12, from bar 84/189, presents the consequent and the cadential element in semiquaver elaboration, having been contaminated, as it were, by the figuration of the previous solo that is itself based on the same two elements. Coincidentally or not, the result closely resembles, in texture and cadential breadth, the ending of the first movement.

Variation and *dénouement*

Variation incorporated earlier in the *tutti* framework is of greater structural significance. Several movements possess a central ritornello that both confirms the key reached in the previous solo and forces the music on to the next tonal level. In most instances, the open period either produces the movement's last excursive tonal step or initiates the end-play. In bars 121–9/231–9 in the finale of No. 8, for example, Vivaldi restores the tonic key simply by reiterating the head-motif, producing an effect of two ritornellos in one. The pertinent point is that a varied *tutti* period helps to enhance the part of the movement of greatest volatility, whether it changes the key or not. When progress away from the tonic key is completed, the ritornello typically alters in function; having served as a stable period that reinforces a modulation, it can now admit some instability, turn the direction of the movement around and thus provoke the end-play. In many concerto movements Vivaldi builds tension towards this *dénouement* by making each of the early ritornellos shorter than the last. It is no coincidence that the first three *tutti* periods in the first movement of No. 10 (*The Hunt*) are of thirty, eighteen and twelve bars respectively, or that the third exhibits a degree of transformation – in the homophonic reduction of the antecedent (bars 112–17) and the subsequent unison phrase derived from bars 22–6 – far greater than that of the second.

Another form of variation, adopted by J. S. Bach for the restoration of F major near the end of the first movement of the second Brandenburg concerto, is the introduction of a motto-like unison version of the antecedent. Examples occur in the third ritornellos of the finale of No. 7 and the first movement of No. 11, functioning as calls to attention in anticipation of the end-play. The unison theme used in isolation at bars 43–6 and 70–3 in the first movement of No. 12 is not a ritornello but a device dividing one part of an episode from its continuation. The result of its interjections – brief passages for the soloist with moments of respite – is important evidence suggesting that the work's principal part was conceived for oboe, not violin.

More radical conversions of ritornello elements can occur. The unison phrase in bars 118–21 in the first movement of No. 10 (*The Hunt*) is based on the local tonic unlike its model, bars 22–6 on the local dominant. An identical reversal of harmonic poles happens in the finale (bars 13–16/184–7 and 115–18/286–9). The *tutti* passages at bars 41–2 and 52–8 in the first movement of No. 7 are of a different order: distinctly less related to the first ritornello than other variants in Op. 8. Doubtless this is a sign of the movement's early vintage; the first of these passages is especially reminiscent of the style of Op. 3 in the way its chromatic progression interrupts the solo period.

The ritornellos of the first movement of No. 8 are exceptionally changeable: one might almost speak of 'ritornello-variation form' in this case. The motif of the antecedent, having already been varied in the initial cadential element, is the basis for three transformations: the sequence in bars 50–2 and two cadential phrases, bars 52–5 and 79–82. We find, too, a new motif at bars 34–5 that relates to no other *tutti* passage in the movement, but its significance is minimal. A cousin of the sequence in bars 16–20 of No. 11, it is a stock chromatic progression of Vivaldi's appearing in many works.[10] It was probably pressed into service here as an easy way of forcing an already wayward progression back to B♭ major.

The new phrase at bars 50–2 of No. 8 is particularly interesting because it is a sequential consequent of the standard type lacking in the initial ritornello. A 'late' sequential consequent similarly crops up in the first movement of No. 11 (bars 94–9). In both cases the ritornello in question is the third, where the sequence contributes a culminating effect to the volatile middle phase of the movement prior to the end-play. Vivaldi's calculation – or the end result, at any rate – relates to his tactic of withdrawing the consequent, considered earlier. On hearing the delayed sequence, the listener might feel, with a sense of *déjà vu*, that it is the ideal continuation that tacitly belonged to the movement's ritornello from the outset. To believe this is to acknowledge that some of Vivaldi's ritornello forms operate progressively to reveal the significance of the ritornello's ideas, whether purely musical or also extra-musical, at points later than the first period. Aspects of *The Four Seasons* can be explained in these terms, as we shall see.

It is instructive at this juncture to examine the framework of *The Storm at Sea* (No. 5): the closest to the *Seasons* of all the remaining works in Op. 8 in terms of its structural peculiarities, and possibly Vivaldi's earliest character-ized concerto. Three principal features absent from Nos. 6–12 may be singled out. One is that the first movement, ending on the dominant, invites the second; the slow movement in turn invites the finale with a traditional Phrygian cadence altered by the Italian sixth. Since Vivaldi had all but rejected the convention of linking movements (commonplace in earlier concertos fashioned from short sections and those, like Handel's, in the Corellian tradition), its use here suggests that some extra-musical idea unfolds through the work. The second feature also helps to maintain a continuous process: in both fast movements, the distinctions between ritornello and episode are frequently blurred. Bars 70–3 in the first movement, for instance, come across more as the transitional core of a ritornello framed by statements of the antecedent (in total, bars 66–77) than as a solo period.

The final feature is that the first period of the finale consists only of an antecedent; further elements are withheld until the second *tutti* period (from bar 77/185), and this, a complex of cadential phrases, does not include a regular consequent. Why this should happen is part of the enigma of Vivaldi's characterized concertos; the extra-musical reason in this instance, if one were ever entertained, will doubtless remain a secret. We can at least recognize the general principle of what may be termed 'progressive ritornello form', in which the ritornello itself is revealed, or radically altered, in piecemeal fashion. The first movements of Nos. 8 and 11, possessing some of the most variable ritornellos in the whole collection, appear to share the same rationale. As in those movements, a 'late' sequential element is introduced to both fast movements of *The Storm at Sea*. One case, bars 174–91/282–99 in the finale, may not seem particularly consequent-like because it lacks a head-motif and is itself the means of transition. Nevertheless, it has a three-bar harmonic rate that complements that of the antecedent; something like it would in theory work well from bar 19/127 in E♭ major, commencing with the tonic chord. The other, bars 43–8 in the first movement, has the circuitous progression and all the spirit one expects of a consequent; it forcefully usurps the role of the feeble original sequence (bars 5–7) from which it is derived, and installs a new, emphatic cadence. By these means the ritornello framework bends, shifting our perception; Vivaldi perhaps hoped that our sense of the tumultuous progress of a sea-storm would change with it.

Tonal schemes

As we have seen, Op. 8 provides much evidence of a movement having three phases – excursion, central volatility, end-play – in which ritornellos and episodes are the means of directing a structure, not whole structural units in themselves. Since the keys visited and the timing of key-change govern and articulate the flow of periods, their distribution over a whole movement might be expected to reflect the three-phase concept.

But let us not suppose that Vivaldi necessarily thought in such terms. He did not compose with the calculation of an architect or possess Bach's genius for proportion and symmetry. His manuscripts show that he (like many composers of his day) typically writes a movement from beginning to end, fluently and quickly, without the aid of sketches. When composing a solo episode, he usually devises new material in a process of more or less constant invention; the type and scope of the figurations themselves tend to dictate both the point when a modulation will occur and the key that might be reached. An episode can thus end up in a new key almost by chance, rather than be directed towards it from the outset, before the composer ever considers what might happen two or three periods further on. The kind of tonal scheme we are considering cannot therefore be regarded as a pre-formed mould in which ritornello form is cast. Whereas binary form and sonata form are typically based on reaching the dominant key and a rondo periodically returns to the tonic, ritornello form lacks a fixed central goal because some of its seemingly strategic keys are arrived at empirically.

It is all the more remarkable, then, that the tonal schemes of Op. 8 show considerable consistency – born not of calculation but of Vivaldi's fine instinct for what seemed right. Their distinctions reveal his equally intuitive search for novel techniques. His experience by *c.* 1720 gave him the only ritornello-form plan he needed: a stretchable and contractable tonal-periodic procedure on which any number of fast movements could be modelled without limiting their individuality. He could leave certain decisions – whether to allow a central ritornello to modulate, for instance – to the inspiration of the moment, knowing that whatever he chose to do could not damage the basic design of the movement.

Example 6 presents the tonal schemes of the fast movements of Nos. 5–12 in a way that allows us to compare their proportions: each is plotted across the staff from 0 to 100 per cent of the movement's duration. White and black notes represent major and minor keys, respectively. Stemmed notes show the location and keys of *tutti* periods; a beamed group thus stands for one that changes key. Stemless notes show the tonal course of solo episodes from the end of the previous *tutti*. Notes printed small represent some of the keys visited only briefly. In key-relationship labels beneath the staves, 'R' stands for relative major, 'r' for relative minor. (Comparison may be made with the schemes of *The Four Seasons*: p. 69.)

The rigidity of each scheme near its beginning and end is immediately apparent. In all cases the use of the tonic key during the final phase – slurs labelled '3' – occupies, on average, the last quarter of the movement. It is almost as axiomatic for the initial excursive phase of the movement to progress first to the dominant key whether the mode of the tonic is major or minor: slurs '1'. In Vivaldi's concertos in general the choice of the relative major or minor key for this part of the strategy is less common than one might imagine. Although no other aspect comes close to being an immutable principle, common trends are not difficult to find. One – a matter more of harmonic resourcefulness than of tonality – is Vivaldi's use of the tonic minor in major-key works. The change of mode is typically employed for the pathos it lends to an end-play: bars 186–97/345–56 in the finale of No. 11, for instance.

Except in the case of the first movement of No. 8 (which has an unorthodox scheme matching its unorthodox ritornellos), the first modulation is not precipitate. It takes place around 25–35 per cent of the way through, following a substantial quantity of music in the tonic key that enhances the sense of its imminence. Vivaldi's acute sense of form is such that there is no significant difference in the proportional location of this modulation between movements such as the finales of Nos. 5 and 9 where the new key is reached in the second solo period and those in which the change occurs in the first. Slightly more delay is caused if, in a 'false transition', the first solo digresses momentarily only to revert to the tonic key, as in the first movement of No. 5. The change itself is typically abrupt, lacking in expressive niceties; it fractures the lyrical continuity of the solo episode in a nakedly functional way, forcing the listener to hear it as a signal heralding the next ritornello. Consider the shift to A minor at bar 37/129 in the finale of No. 7: Example 7. In an instant it breaks into the sequence, making the phrasing irregular and forcing the harmony to the dominant; thus it provokes the cadence that draws the *tutti* passage.

After the first tonal step, the number and choice of internal keys, the timing of their introduction and the functions of *tutti* and solo periods in the progression vary considerably: slurs '2' in Example 6. Both movements of No. 12 and the first of No. 9 have in common a 'pure' procedure in which a second key-change and the return to the tonic are each achieved in the same way as the first modulation: as a direct step in an episode, affirmed by a ritornello. In this way, the tonal pattern correlates precisely with the pattern of *tutti*–solo alternation.

In other cases the second phase is more complex: the relationship of the music to the tonic key, hitherto very close, is slackened distinctly and sometimes undermined. Whereas in the first movement of No. 12 the mediant E minor occurs in tertiary relationship to both the dominant and tonic, the use of the same key in the first movement of No. 6 is insulated from the immediate tonal sphere of the tonic. Arising out of a lengthy passage in the relative minor, and influenced also by the visit at bar 41 to D minor, it comes across more as the dominant minor of A minor than the mediant of C major. Its independence of the tonic key is such that the arrival of C major at bar 65, after the briefest of transitions, does not sound like the return we await: after this the full end-play apparatus is indispensable as the means by which the tonic key regains its status.

The schemes of the finales of Nos. 7 and 9 are similar; in both cases the second phase is distanced from the tonic, D minor, by progression into the parallel region of the relative major, F, via the latter's dominant key. The juxtaposition of the two tonal spheres and both the brevity and location within the piece of the second phase remind us of *da capo* form and the ternary schemes of Corelli. No. 7 has, from bar 92/184, a recapitulation of the solo passage heard at the outset that imposes the tonic key at precisely the point corresponding to the reprise of the 'A'-section in the aria structure. (Vivaldi manages only with difficulty to resist a second excursion to the dominant: bars 104–10/196–202.) This manner of restoring the tonic, through hiatus at a

Example 6   Tonal schemes: fast movements of Nos. 5–12

Example 6 (*cont.*)

Example 7   No. 7, III, bars 32–43 (violin parts omitted)

cadence, is an old technique. Although it is rare in Op. 8, Vivaldi would later employ it regularly to exit from the tonal *impasse* created by the second phase; nine out of the twenty-four fast movements of Op. 9 feature it.

In the first movement of No. 7 and the finales of Nos. 8 and 11, the tonic key is restored within an open *tutti* period. At the point where the excursive tendency of the tonal progression gives way to the recursive one, it is natural for the original roles of episode and ritornello – tonal change and tonal affirmation, respectively – to be abandoned or even reversed. Vivaldi appears to pursue this notion further when an open ritornello modulates not to the tonic but to a third new key: a move that offsets the second phase as a passage of development distinct from the movement's opening and closing stages. Consider, for instance, the fifth period of both the finale of No. 6 and the first movement of No. 10: see Table 2. The change of key in each case is sudden, and cannot be regarded as a necessary or even logical stepping-stone back to the tonic key. A sense of the new key being the culmination of the tonal progress of the second phase, rather than the result of a third – and late – excursive step, is especially clear in the first movement of *The Hunt*. The key in question, G minor, is prefaced by a lengthy passage in its dominant, D minor, and telegraphed at bar 106. Small wonder that C minor, from bar 107, has the character of a subdominant key as if G minor were the tonic.

A similar C-to-G 'plagal' orientation pervades the second phase in the finale of the same work, but with an important difference: G minor is imposed in the second ritornello, not arrived at later. Vivaldi was not often inclined, so

Table 2

		No. 6 *Pleasure*, III:				No. 10 *The Hunt*, I:	
	Scoring	Bars	Key		Scoring	Bars	Key
1:	T	1–29	C ⎤	⎡ T		1–31	B♭
2:	S	29–53	C–G	phase 1	S	31–64	B♭–F
3:	T	53–71	G ⎦	⎣ T		64–82	F
4:	S	71–95	G–a ⎤	phase 2 ⎡ S		82–112	F–d–c
5:	T	95–107	a–d ⎦	⎣ T		112–24	c–g
6:	S	107–45	d–C	return	S	124–50	g–B♭
7:	T	145–66	C		T		150–62	B♭

early in a movement, to give the function of excursive modulation to a *tutti* period. Sudden and emphatic, the shift at bar 71/242 is the clearest evidence we have seen so far that the composer sensed a need to mark the second phase as a passage distinct from the first. Behind this rare feature, one imagines, might lie an extra-musical idea about the progress of the hunt itself. In a parallel case, the full band imposes C minor, and installs the usurping consequent, during the second ritornello in *The Storm at Sea* (I, bars 39–51) – the period containing the movement's most tempestuous music. Here, too, the target key proves to be G minor.

These instances suggest that Vivaldi would frequently select a second-phase key for its own sake, irrespective of its relationship to the tonic. His choice, like that of the tonic key initially, is likely to be a subjective response to the key's strong contextual association with the motivic and harmonic fabric of his invention. G minor, for instance, might be used exclusively for its individual character and colour in a way that can be replicated elsewhere in a work with a different tonic key. The orientation to G minor, with or without C minor as an accomplice, is quite possibly a feature of all four fast movements of *The Storm at Sea* (in E♭) and *The Hunt* (in B♭) because the key itself represents something implicit in the themes of both works: anxiety, perhaps, in the face of the storm and the pursuit of the hunt. *Summer*, too, helps us to appreciate that G minor and its relatives C minor and D minor were Vivaldi's palette for pictures of Nature's violence and man's unease. We will return, in Chapters 4 and 6, to the apparent semiotic significance of particular keys.

Episodes

Although Vivaldi's solo passages tend to be valued for the virtuosity and surface expression that we, as listeners, most readily perceive, their influence on the structure of a fast movement is considerable. Their relationship to the *tutti* framework is symbiotic: without them, most ritornello-form manoeuvres apparent in Op. 8 would not exist. What is remarkable is how strong that relationship can be when episodes – in Op. 8, at least – have such slight thematic connection with the ritornellos. In most fast movements in Nos. 5–12, new motifs and violinistic figures of little or no thematic consequence are introduced and just as freely abandoned in ever-changing solo periods. Italian composers typically preferred variations in figuration and texture as the principal means, besides key-change, of writing at length, but this does not explain why Vivaldi tended to eschew thematic significance in solos. Even if he had known, as we know from the ritornello forms of J. S. Bach, how fast movements that are both long and densely integrated thematically could successfully be composed, there is no reason to suppose that he would have adopted any habit that would blur his crystal-clear distinctions between episode and ritornello in solo-concerto form.

Vivaldi knew something that is unlikely ever to have dawned on Bach. He understood that, although flights of invention and feats of virtuosity momentarily distract the ear, these very distractions are, paradoxically, a principal means of structural cohesion. By their restlessness and novelty, the episodes offset the ritornellos whose attributes are stability and familiarity; by drawing attention away from the ritornello they increase the significance of its recurrence and thus underpin the long-term function of the *tutti* framework.

Thirteen distinct solo figures appear in the first movement of No. 10 (*The Hunt*): on average, each is used for seven bars – about nine seconds in performance. Table 3 shows their distribution over the three episodes and the extent of their relationship with music introduced beforehand. Reference to the ritornello is minimal; the 'stamping' motif in bars 131, 133 and 135 is used merely to articulate phrases of 'k' consisting otherwise of scalar semiquavers. Melodic relationships are meagre since almost every figure has a new contour. The real bond between these ideas – preventing each episode from being a loose cannon likely to damage the structural integrity of the music – is their rhythmic uniformity featuring triplet quavers (a, c, d, g and h) and patterns of repeated quavers derived from the ritornello (b, e, f and i). Vivaldi has

Table 3

Episode	Figure	Bars	Melodic relationship	Rhythmic relationship
1:	a	31–3		
	b	34–41		ritornello
	c	42–8	arpeggio = a	a
	d	49–54		a, c
	e	55–63		ritornello, b
2:	f	82–93	double-stopping = e	
	g	94–9	arpeggio = a (inversion)	a, c, d
	h	100–11		a, c, d, g
3:	i	124–7	double-stopping = e, f	f
	j	128–9		
	k	130–6	ritornello	ritornello, j, m
	l	137–42		
	m	143–9	variant of k	k

differentiated between *tutti* and solo periods as much as he dared, using little more than rhythm to protect the structure from disintegration.

Actual thematic relationships between episodes are scarce. We have seen, in the finale of No. 7, the opening of the first episode recalled in the last, but this is very rare in Op. 8. Particular figures crop up in two or more passages, but not regularly. An unusual instance concerns the finale of No. 6, where a descending motif, appearing in every episode, helps to mark the movement's tonal progression: bars 39, 45, 86, 112 and 130. Only the first movement of No. 9 has episodes designed to be thoroughly alike, presumably because the principal idea, with its chaconne-like descending bass, is ideal for repetition: Example 8a. Related in its syncopation to the ritornello, the motif spawns variants in F major and A minor (8c and d), an elaborated version (b) and a truncated, 'Neapolitan' phrase (e). The episodes are further related by their scalar and broken-chord figurations.

Besides rhythmic uniformity, *tutti* framing and tonal direction, other factors hold episodes together in cases of figurative diversity. One is the phrasing of

Example 8 No. 9, I (a) bars 22–6; (b) bars 87–90;
(c) bars 45–7; (d) bars 69–71; (e) bars 102–4

the episode itself – a construction often based on much the same formal principles as those Vivaldi applies to a ritornello. The first two solos in No. 6 (*Pleasure*), for instance, each begin with an antecedent–consequent pair of phrases: a definitive shape that directs one's attention forward to the next change of key while acting as a strait-jacket that restricts the disruptive effect of freely introduced figures. Another factor that gives structural sense to an episode is the contour of the principal part – commonly an arc as exemplified in the third solo period of No. 6. Most importantly, the sequence of episodes is allied to the ebb and flow of a movement's structure as a whole. Generally speaking, solos early in the movement are highly stereotyped formulas designed to achieve modulatory steps. Episodes belonging to the second, developmental phase are typically less formalized, more animated in their figurations, and tonally more digressive. It is at this stage, too, that distinctions between solo and *tutti* scoring tend to be minimized; the second episodes in the fast movements of No. 11 each culminate in a substantial transition involving the whole band in thematic reference. Having become freer, Vivaldi's episodic writing generally reaches its most rhapsodic state during the movement's end-play, although extreme expression of boldly extrovert or plaintive kinds is not always included.

The old convention of quoting a movement's head-motif at the beginning of the first solo, as shown in the first movement of No. 7, is something Vivaldi would continue to adopt occasionally. Bars 114–26 in the first movement of

No. 11 demonstrate other options: of adding solo figuration to a ritornello and deriving an episodic passage from an earlier *tutti* theme. But thematic cross-references between episodes and ritornellos are few in Op. 8 and of uneven distribution throughout the composer's mature solo concertos in general simply because they are neither essential nor necessarily very helpful to a compositional method that normally makes a virtue out of *tutti*–solo disparity.

In short, the integrity of fast-movement forms in Op. 8 depends far more on an optimum coalescence of structural units than on a 'thematic process'. Most intriguing of all is the way that those units often have three parts, and that a set of three units might serve as the next larger unit. Many ritornellos, and some episodes too, contain three elements. Three periods, *tutti*–solo–*tutti*, are the basic unit of a tonal phase, while three phases together constitute the ground-plan of the movement. And we can have little doubt, having identified some of the relationships between a work's first movement and its finale, that Vivaldi strove for a degree of unity by design over the largest unit of all: the three-movement concerto itself.

4

Expression and meaning

It would be difficult to instance an eighteenth-century instrumental collection that satisfies more successfully than Vivaldi's Op. 8 the ideal aesthetic propounded by Francesco Geminiani: 'The Intention of Musick is not only to please the Ear, but to express Sentiments, strike the Imagination, affect the Mind, and command the Passions'.[1] Vivaldi, himself an exceptionally accomplished violinist, would doubtless have satisfied patrons and audiences if the only merits of his concertos were the spectator-sport of impressive virtuosity and orchestral dynamism of an abstract quality. But in this respect he was far from being Corelli's successor. With so many of his concertos one senses that he was incapable of writing 'pure' music devoid of the passions of the human spirit. His experience as a composer of dramatic vocal music has much to do with this, but it is not the only factor.

Commentators have naturally regarded Op. 8 as the clearest manifestation of Vivaldi's concern for extra-musical meaning, in recognition of both the programmatic nature of *The Four Seasons* and the concentration of works with titles in the set as a whole. All too often it has been the directly descriptive passages that have commanded attention to the neglect of the wider musical context in which they exist. This is not to decry the bird-songs, winds and storms that abound in several works: depictions, highly original for Italian instrumental composition, that occupy an important historical position between those in Johann Jakob Walther's violin pieces and Beethoven's 'Pastoral' Symphony. But it would be wrong to regard them as the real substance of Vivaldi's invention or attribute to them alone the lasting success of his music.

It was inevitable that such expressions – initially fascinating novelties that pall on becoming familiar – would fall foul of critical opinion. When judged to be less than subtle or too realistic they were summarily dismissed; Geminiani doubtless counted Vivaldi among the 'Professors of Legerdemain and Posture-masters' who purveyed the naïve musical imitations of which he complained.[2] In France, where artistic representations of nature were much in vogue, Vivaldi's descriptive music came under attack, conversely, for being not realistic enough: ' . . . in Vivaldi's *Primavera* he [the unprejudiced listener] would find only shepherd dances which are common to all seasons, and where consequently spring is no more represented than summer or fall'.[3] Marc Pincherle's rebuttal – 'If we are given good music, the accuracy of the imitation will come as a bonus' – is telling, but even his discourse on Vivaldi as a 'descriptive musician', though in many respects the finest in modern literature, falls into the trap of exalting the composer's powers of depiction over his sensibilities to the implications of what is depicted.[4]

Recent studies have done much to redress this imbalance, recognizing the close figurative relationship between particular arias and concerto movements and assessing the symbology of the instrumental works with titles.[5] Many precedents for extra-musical allusions and programmatic depictions existed: the tradition of the *chasse*, music on the subject of the seasons (Christopher Simpson, Lully, Johann Caspar Ferdinand Fischer), on natural phenomena such as storms (Locke, Campra, Marais), and on other special themes – the Mystery Sonatas of Biber, for instance, or the character-pieces of the French *clavecinistes*.[6] Vivaldi's interest in such things is likely to have been inspired initially by the descriptive violin music of the Austrian school; of the many cuckoos that inhabit Western music, that in Biber's *Sonata representativa* is probably the closest to Vivaldi's own (Example 9).[7] But a compositional aesthetic, applicable to a whole concerto rather than a mere passage, solidified only when realistic imagery came regularly to convey the *affetti* of arias in operas, cantatas and serenatas. As Cesare Fertonani points out,[8] a high concentration of mimetic and naturalistic expressions informs Vivaldi's opera *Arsilda, regina di Ponto* (RV 700) of 1716 – precisely the time when he began to make explicit reference, through titles, to similar allusions in concertos. His departure finds an echo in Venetian painting, particularly in the 'Storm at Sea' and evocative seasonal landscapes of Marco Ricci (1676–1730), in which small human figures are overwhelmed by the effects, benign or malign, of Nature. In music, other characterized pieces would follow, including Christoph Graupner's *Die vier Jahreszeiten* (1733), Lorenzo Gaetano Zavateri's *Concerto a Tempesta di mare* (Op. 1 No. 12, 1735),[9] Pietro Locatelli's *Il pianto d'Arianna* (Op. 7 No. 6, 1741), Francesco Durante's *Le quattro stagioni dell'anno* (1747) and his concerto entitled *La pazzia* ('Madness').

There is a difference, of course, between *The Four Seasons* or *La notte* ('Night'), where actual depictions are explained by captions or movement-titles, and *The Storm at Sea*, *Pleasure*, *The Hunt* and several other concertos for which the only verbal clue to what is represented is the title of the whole

Example 9   (a) Biber, *Sonata representativa*, bars 78–81
(b) Vivaldi, *Summer*, I, bars 31–4

work. But is it very great in terms of how we perceive the music? It is a distinction in the degree to which Vivaldi helps us to associate sounds with certain meanings, but the absence of his assistance on a passage-to-passage basis does not imply that the music lacks meaning. In any case, he did not set out to explain in words all that his music can express. Even *The Four Seasons*, for all their literary annotations, leave several passages for the listener to interpret unaided and the overall significance and consequences of certain depicted events to be imagined. In these works, the sum of their individual depictions remains a series of scantily connected ideas; it is the perceived flavour of the concerto as a whole, not the depictions by themselves, that inspires and fixes in the listener's mind a single impression of the season in question. If we accept that Vivaldi hoped that *Winter* would convey a sense of how exhilarating winter-time can be, we may suppose that his intention for, say, No. 5 was identical: an impression of the nature and effects of a sea-storm that comes as much from the listener's imagination as from the appositeness of the music. In these terms, the specified descriptive episodes in *Winter* – the cracking of ice, the chattering of teeth and so forth – are indeed Pincherle's 'bonus'.

We should equally question the difference between Vivaldi's concertos with titles and the vast majority lacking them. There seems after all to be no marked distinction between Op. 8 Nos. 6 and 12, for instance, though the former is named *Pleasure*. Since each contains a 'bitter-sweet' slow movement between lively, 'agreeable' fast movements in C major, it might appear that the title 'Il piacere' was appended as an afterthought. It is not impossible that Vivaldi sometimes composed 'plain' concertos *before* opting to give them characterizing titles. Distinct shades of ink in the autograph manuscript concordant with No. 10 show that he added the words 'La Caccia' to his standard heading, 'Con[cer]to [space] Del Viualdi', after he had drafted at least the first page or two of the music – or conceivably after the whole work had been notated (see Plate 3).[10] Whereas the hunt-finale of *Autumn* was written to suit a predetermined idea, the title of *The Hunt* was perhaps chosen, aptly enough, to describe existing music.

The implication could scarcely be more astonishing: any concerto had the potential to be characterized while Vivaldi composed it or to be seen afterwards to possess a characterization. Although it would be absurd to pretend that every untitled work is steeped in extra-musical meaning (the low frequency of those with titles speaks for itself), it follows that such infusions that exist must be recognizable to a degree. Let us therefore equalize the works of Op. 8 by ignoring descriptive titles and obviously depictive passages. What forms of expression remain, and to what extent are they meaningful beyond purely musical considerations?

The soloist's contribution

The principal part cannot, by itself, convey a single idea or mood representative of an entire fast movement or the whole concerto. In Op. 8, Vivaldi acknowledges as much by rarely deviating from the practice of writing episodes consisting of freely introduced figures. Since solo passages impose themselves in the aural foreground of the music and, in fast movements, are not continuous, any extra-musical notions implicit in them can only be isolated facets of a work's overall character or theme. The few elements that do recur can, however, override each episode's transience. We observed in Chapter 3 how rhythmic uniformity is particularly important as the means of imbuing the disparate figurations in *The Hunt* with a common feeling of animation – clearly an attribute on which the work's title was based.

Since Vivaldi evidently regarded virtuosity as a paramount feature of solos, any idea of characterizing the episodes would normally have been subservient to this or non-existent. Even in *The Four Seasons* there are moments – bars 26–33 in *Winter*, for instance – when the fulsomeness of the display almost blocks out the sense we are encouraged by the sonnet to associate with it. Nevertheless, in many works the two functions are shown to be compatible within the unfolding 'plot' of a fast movement's structure. Most common is the characterization of a final, cadenza-like episode as a *dénouement*, tinged with regret, that arrives after – or, in dramatic terms, as the result of – the volatility of the movement's second phase. In this respect bars 186–99/345–58 of the finale of No. 11 share something of the meaning of the countryman's lament in *Summer* (I, bars 116–54). The passage is no less virtuosic than earlier episodes, but the nature of the virtuosity is radically transformed, with plaintive Neapolitan harmonies in D minor, into the antithesis of what it had been. After this, the final ritornello further cements this classic opposition of ethos and pathos.

Sometimes a movement is distinguished by particular violin techniques common to two or more episodes; *The Four Seasons* show, with rapid scales representing violent gusts of wind, for instance, that this is an important method of communicating recurrent ideas. The finale of No. 7 could be said to be specially characterized by its pervasive double-stopping, or that of No. 8 by its two cadenzas with broken chords over a dominant pedal, no matter how much the result defies definition as an extra-musical concept.

Thematic and figurative correlations

Vivaldi turned time and time again to favourite expressions – stock phrases, certainly, though their recurrence suggests that they are not without significance as rhetorical or representational devices. Common to many of the composer's works of the 1710s and 1720s is a melodic descent of four conjunct notes, usually from dominant to supertonic or from tonic to dominant. More than two dozen cases appear in Op. 8 outside *The Four Seasons*, taking a variety of guises from *tutti* motifs in ritornellos to simple and decorated solo phrases: Examples 8a and 10 give a small selection. So widespread a feature alone accounts for much of the colouring of the collection. Few fast movements lack it (its absence entirely from No. 8 is exceptional) and even the slow movement of No. 12, quoted in Example 13a, is based on the same contour.

Although the descending notes seem regularly to be a by-product of Vivaldi's tendency to write upper parts over a pedal, and although they govern a tonic-to-dominant progression of universal usage when adopted in the bass (in the ritornello of the finale of No. 7, for instance), there can be little doubt that they were sometimes purposefully selected to be an actual theme of representational potential. A particularly high concentration of cases in *The Four Seasons* (a factor we will examine in Chapter 6) is not the only evidence of this. Thematic status is implicit in the choice of the descent for principal elements in the ritornellos of the first movements of *The Hunt* and No. 12 and the finale of *The Storm at Sea*. In the last case, the motivic significance of the descending antecedent (bars 1–18, E♭–D–C–B♭) is underpinned by the ascending melodic shape of the delayed consequent, into which Vivaldi was clearly at pains to squeeze the four-note series in retrograde (Example 11).[11] The same descent provides also the episodic motif in the finale of *Pleasure* whose recurrence correlates to the movement's tonal scheme (see p. 47). Precisely what extra-musical significance it carries is anyone's guess. Perhaps

Example 10   (a) No. 10, I, bars 22–7; (b) No. 12, I, bars 5–9;
(c) No. 7, III, bars 95–9; (d) No. 11, I, bars 59–63

Example 11   No. 5, III, bars 77–85/185–93

its 'meaning' – as a kind of 'floating' leitmotif – is entirely illusory; one suspects that Vivaldi instinctively felt only that discrete passages 'strike the imagination' all the more for being linked by it.

The first movement of No. 10 (*The Hunt*) is particularly rich in apparent allusions recognizable from *The Four Seasons* and *The Storm at Sea*. The hunting-horn calls of bars 34–41, for instance, have much the same rhythm and 'primitive' tonic and dominant alternation as the hunt-finale of *Autumn* (from bar 14). These movements also share triplet arpeggio figures of a kind, in fast triple metre, that suggests the quarry's flight and the galloping pursuit. Descending *tutti* scales in bars 94–9 of No. 10, occurring in the volatile second phase of the movement, compare with those in the first movement of *Autumn* (bars 44–8). Later, solo flourishes in bars 130–7, each strongly articulated by a *tutti* motif, are the equivalent of similarly animated phrases in the first movements of *Spring* and *The Storm at Sea* and the finales of *Summer*, *Autumn* and *Winter*.

Vivaldi's use of particular figurations appears in many cases to have been triggered by his choice of key. It is surely not merely coincidental that bars 53–66 in *The Storm at Sea* – the work's most sustained allusion to the violence of a tempest – progress from C minor to G minor. Here, on-beat scales featured before this point are abandoned in favour of descending scales, beginning on off-beat semiquavers, that are identical in kind to those that pervade the G minor finale of *Summer*. One must also reckon that such characteristically Vivaldian string textures are not universal in application. In Op. 8, tremolo passages are confined to *The Four Seasons* and *The Storm at Sea*, and rapid scales to these works and *The Hunt*, because they are synonymous with animated events.[12]

Accompaniments and harmony

It is already clear that Vivaldi's handling of accompaniments during episodes is to a large extent an indication of a passage's significance. The critical factors are the density of scoring, the degree to which the whole ensemble interjects, and the use of figures specific to a movement's character. Unlike the majority of episodes where the soloist is accompanied in plain fashion by the continuo alone or one or more of the violin and viola parts, passages involving all instruments in motivic exchanges (bars 68–85 of No. 11, for instance, or bars 55–71/147–63 of the finale of No. 7) give climactic depth to the second phase of a movement in much the same way as the onslaught of winds causes change in *Summer*.

Just as certain figures and textures readily transfer – with their associated implications – from one work to another, particular harmonic formulas seem to recur because they are representational devices. Like embedded subliminal images that, though fleeting, can strongly dictate how film sequences are perceived, they have a marked influence on the listener from within Vivaldi's routine progressions that helps to determine the character of an entire movement. The parallel thirds often associated with the four-note descent, described above, are an example of such a signal, albeit a variable one. Much of Vivaldi's string writing relies, indeed, on the natural harmoniousness of parallel thirds as a means of evoking one mood or another.

Mention has been made already of the antithetical pathos communicated by Neapolitan-sixth chords in certain minor-key passages. In such contexts (No. 11, III, bars 190–4/349–53, for example) Vivaldi milks the strangeness of the diminished-third interval for all its worth. More traditional is his use of harmony over a chromatic bass, though he is more inclined than other

Example 12   (a) *Spring*, I, bar 3;
(b) *Autumn*, I, bar 3; (c) No. 12, I, bar 2

composers to introduce this plaintive device unexpectedly as a sudden contradiction of a joyous mood: see bars 17–19/139–41 in the finale of *Spring*.

Metrical and tonal parameters

A favourite harmonic signal in major-key movements is the seventh chord built on the raised subdominant, often in false relations to the previous chord, in initial imperfect cadences common to *Pleasure* (Example 1a), *Spring*, *Autumn* and No. 12 (Example 12). We readily equate this Vivaldian thumbprint with experiences of delight, but what we sense is not merely cadential satisfaction. The special chord is a momentary symptom of a longer-term musical characterization that is fully established even by the time the second bar of each piece is heard: one created by a particularly potent mix of key, metre, tempo and rhythm.

We have arrived at the nub of the issue: that the mood or character of a fast movement is largely predetermined by Vivaldi's choice of the parameters in which the initial ritornello will be set. There is a world of difference, in terms of harmonic rhythm and its energy, between the common-time Allegro of moderate pace (a ubiquitous movement-type today widely known as the 'concerto Allegro') and fast movements in 2/4, 3/4 and 3/8 metres. But – as has been hinted several times in Chapter 3 and above – it is chiefly Vivaldi's selection of a key that superimposes on a metrical type the potential for the music to exude a particular sense with associated figurative content. It is scarcely remarkable that some musicians of the period felt that each key possessed its own ethos suited to the arousal of specific affections. What is remarkable in Vivaldi's case is that such a view made an easy transition from opera to textless concerto, and that he seems sometimes to have attributed an ethos to a key irrespective of its local function. In other words: a key might retain an absolute semiotic significance whether adopted as a tonic key or used inside a movement's tonal scheme.

Pincherle was the first to note that C major, neither a common tonality for concertos in general nor a particularly natural one for violinists, is by far the composer's most frequent choice of tonic key.[13] And if the fact suggests that Vivaldi was enamoured of the 'agreeableness' that characterizes Op. 8 Nos. 6 and 12, the high frequency of G minor – both as a tonic and as an internal choice – must betray his preoccupation with ideas of anxiety, chaos, danger and lament. The regular appearance of tempestuous scales or other agitated figures in many G minor concertos – *Night* (RV 104), RV 156 and RV 577, for instance – concurs in a meaningful way with Vivaldi's use of the same key for arias of vengeance, horror or pessimism.[14] A comparable uniformity of manner may be heard in concertos set in tonic keys adopted less frequently. The gravity of D minor, remarked upon in Chapter 3, is usually quite distinctive, while works in A major (a species notably lacking in Op. 8) possess an aggressive brashness typified by *The Cuckoo* RV 335. C minor, though fairly rare as a concerto's tonic key, appears to the same extent as G minor as an internal key in *The Hunt* and *The Storm at Sea*; when used as a dark corollary of G minor it perhaps equates to 'despair'. For *The Four Seasons*, the composer's most sustained essay in key-association in the field of the concerto, the rare tonic keys of E major and F minor occur in ideal juxtaposition with G minor and F major (see p. 68).

In reading meanings into Vivaldi's keys we find ourselves in a minefield of supposition and subjective response. We cannot assume that he attributed specific affections to keys with the dogmatism of some contemporary German and French theorists. One must reckon also that distinctions of string-playing timbre in different keys (arising from the availability, or not, of open strings), besides the characteristic pitches in which wind instruments were designed, were as responsible for the formation of his associations as intervallic differences between scales and notions transferred from opera. Certainly, a particular key did not necessarily mean only one thing to him.[15] C minor, for instance, might represent 'despair' in some places but 'hope' in others (the slow movement of *Il sospetto* RV 199, for example): since the difference lies in the figurative fabric of the music, the two contexts are not contradictory. A parallel may be observed in the method of Johann David Heinichen (1683–1729), who resided in Italy from 1710 to 1716, mostly in Venice where his two operas of 1712–13 preceded Vivaldi's first season as impresario of the same theatre, S. Angelo, by only a few months. In *Der General-Bass in der*

Composition (1728), Heinichen rejects the views of his friend Johann Mattheson and others who had attributed characters to keys on the basis of unequal temperament, but concedes that certain keys are more suitable than others for expressing particular affections.[16] His stance is somewhat under-stated, for among the book's demonstrations of the application of rhetorical devices to aria-composition may be found several key-associations that have a familiar ring: bold, furious figures in D major; 'quarrelsome' ones in A major; pompous heroism and the 'pursuit' of fortune in B♭ major; distress in E minor; anxiety in G minor; amorousness in G major; and flirtation richly aglow in E major.[17] At an earlier date and without the aid of vocal texts, Vivaldi had demonstrated a similarly acute appreciation of the symbiotic relationship between key and figurative invention.

5

The slow movements

Vivaldi's slow movements, of which those in Op. 8 are a reasonably representative selection, have many characteristics in common. Most are also quite brief, and many are extremely plain in their notated form: one might conclude that the composer took only a token interest in them, regarding each merely as a necessary mechanism for separating fast movements. Such a view would be unjust, not least because it fails to take into account the considerable responsibility normally conferred on the soloist for creating the expressive substance of the music – a cherished custom that could continue only if the designs of pieces remained limited in scope. For this reason, Vivaldi, like most composers of his generation, confined himself largely to conventional types of slow movement propagated in repertories, including those of vocal music, that involved improvised virtuosity. His originality with respect to slow movements therefore lies far more in subtleties of musical vocabulary than in structural design.

The most common type of slow movement in Op. 8 is a through-composed one represented in *Spring*, *Winter*, *Pleasure*, No. 9 and No. 11 – and *Summer* too, if one discounts the movement's *presto* interjections. The idea that a single slow movement should be a self-contained centre-piece in a three-movement work was well established, having been a principal characteristic of the Venetian concerto since the beginning of the century. There exist many fine precedents, including Alessandro Marcello's oboe concerto in D minor and Albinoni's Op. 9 No. 2 besides several examples in Vivaldi's *L'estro armonico* Op. 3, for a procedure that proved immensely influential; Handel's admiration for it is evident from his *concerto grosso* Op. 3 No. 2. All cases present a cantabile melody, typically of marked serenity, that invites extempore elaboration – whether notated plainly, as in *Spring* and *Summer*, or with a modicum of ornamental figures. Vivaldi normally provides a mesmeric mono-figurative accompaniment that is more evocative than the melody itself of the music's atmosphere and character. In all the present examples except that of No. 9, this involves the upper strings, with or without the continuo group.[1]

Only in No. 6 is the whole melody sandwiched between initial and closing phrases for the *ripieno* players alone, though this is a framing device Vivaldi had often employed previously: in Op. 3 No. 11, for instance. He realized – as would J. S. Bach with such great intensity in the slow movement of his violin concerto in E major – that a motto-like framing phrase serves to punctuate sentences of the through-composed structure and also furnishes ideal motifs for an ostinato accompaniment. The motto in No. 6, which recurs strategically to affirm the dominant minor key and the return of the tonic, possesses a classic design: a descent to the dominant answered in the same insistent rhythm by an ascent to a perfect cadence, played in octave unison throughout. Vivaldi eschews framing when his accompaniment is purely figurative rather than thematic; the slow movement of No. 11, in which the solo is prefaced by a rather nondescript phrase that does not recur, is something of a hybrid.

Nos. 7, 10 (*The Hunt*) and 12 have movements in binary form: the standard structure for dances and many preludes in *sonate da camera*, employed to some extent also in church sonatas and concertos such as those by Corelli. Two examples, like many others among Vivaldi's concertos, have an intimate two-part scoring that further suggests their generic relationship to the sonata. The accompaniment in the case of No. 7, although for the full band, is more like a kind of amplified continuo support than the figurative backdrop to be seen elsewhere. Here Vivaldi provides merely the bones of the solo part, leaving the flesh to the creative flair of the violinist; in contrast, decorative figures that are integral to the melodic design appear in Nos. 10 and 12. We may note in this connection that Vivaldi sometimes intervened very heavily to limit the performer's prized art of 'gracing the Adagio'; in several slow movements elsewhere – that of the bassoon concerto RV 489 is a good example – intricate embellishments are prescribed to the fullest possible extent.

The slow movements of Nos. 7 and 12 evince a further link with the sonata, being *sarabande* in all but name. The recurring two-bar rhythmic unit in No. 7 regularly appears in Vivaldi's *sonate da camera*: in the *Sarabanda* of RV 17a and the *Preludio* of RV 759, for instance. Likewise, the second-beat stresses in No. 12 are a feature of the *sarabande* in the sonatas RV 754 and 756, among many others. As the traditional distinctions in function between church and court pieces broke down, the characteristics of particular movement-types tended to be transferred from one medium of instrumental music to another. In concertos, the manner of the *sarabanda* – and of the French *sarabande* too, in Handel's *concerti grossi* and other works that are not purely Italianate – lies at the heart of innumerable slow movements presumably because composers saw that it conveniently contrasted in both tempo and metre with the fast movements they most frequently adopted: those in common time. It also offered a lyrical medium capable of being freely adapted; the slow movement of *Spring*, possessing the melodic language of the *sarabanda* but not its form, is one such product.

We are left with three slow movements in Op. 8 that do not conform to either of the two general types described above. The most unusual piece – though its expression is not actually unique within Vivaldi's output – is the solo-less representation of somnolence in *Autumn*, examined in context in the next chapter. In stark contrast to its adjacent fast movements, the Largo of No. 8 harks back to earlier traditions. By framing a through-composed solo with *tutti* phrases, Vivaldi has dressed up an old-fashioned contrapuntal manner in modern clothes. The style – seemingly aimless wanderings through a tonal labyrinth, especially in the first phrase – compares with that of the Adagio in Albinoni's concerto Op. 7 No. 2 (1715).[2]

As noted in Chapter 3, the Largo of *The Storm at Sea* (No. 5) is a special, open-ended construction: a significant interlude between the 'events' of the work's fast movements. It approximates in several respects to an accompanied recitative: it unfolds dramatically with increasing tension; its solo part is a highly declamatory soliloquy of almost hysterical gestures rather than graceful lyricism; and the band articulates the harmonic progression largely by interjecting at the ends of the soloist's phrases.[3] It is not, however, as direct an evocation of recitative as the *Grave recitativo* of the violin concerto RV 208.[4]

Songs without words

It should not surprise us that Vivaldi adopted in his instrumental works a vocal and quasi-dramatic idiom such as this, given that his preoccupation for most of his career was the composition and production of operas. He frequently transferred music from opera to concerto or vice versa,[5] and, as suggested in Chapter 4, imbued his concertos with evocative tonal and figurative colours of the kinds that enhance emotion and meaning in dramatic vocal music. His instincts were for rationalization where technical parallels existed; since ritornellos and accompaniments were required in both arias and concerto movements, these features could serve both contexts in much the same way. In the Largo of *Spring*, the figurative representation of the murmurings of leafy branches and plants is no different in essence from the treatment any composer of *opera seria* might consider giving to references to nature contained in simile arias.

But the influence of aria-composition ran deeper still. Many of Vivaldi's slow

Example 13   (a) No. 12, II;
(b) *Farnace* (RV 711), Act II scene 13

instrumental movements demonstrate one of the most fundamental aspects of his musical language: a certain phraseology and melodic syntax that arises from the prosody of Italian dramatic verse. Phrasing in the Largo of No. 12 is mirrored in the setting – an Allegro – of 'Lascierò d'esser spietato' in *Farnace* (1727): Example 13.[6] We note, in particular, the feminine cadence that accommodates the stressed penultimate syllable and weak final syllable of the last word in the line ('spie*ta*to'). We note, too, that the metrical similarity between such phrases can exist irrespective of marked distinctions in tempo.

The Adagio of *The Hunt*, so simple and disjointed in its regular one-bar phrasing, is the clearest manifestation in Op. 8 of the phonic influence of an imaginary vocal text. Similar phrases, each bearing a single line of text, occur in many of Vivaldi's arias in common time or 2/4 metre, both fast and slow; their endings, and whether they begin with an anacrusis or not, depend on the number and accentuation of syllables in the line. Example 14 quotes from two such pieces; the bass in the second case is phrased with the solo part, with rests, in a manner similar to that of *The Hunt*.

It is not difficult to understand how and why melody of this type transferred to the instrumental realm. In a great number of arias of the period, the ritornello and the singer's first entry begin with the same phrase. Once it became second nature for composers to conceive instrumental openings according to how the first line or two of the text would be set, it was inevitable that the same creative process would permeate purely instrumental music. But although the largely syllabic manner of text-setting shown in Example 14 was applied to slow, medium-paced and fast arias alike, its manifestation in concertos is largely confined to slow movements. As we saw in Chapter 3, fast movements rely on quite different formal procedures with solos in an instrumental idiom to which disjointed phrasing and feminine cadencing are foreign. For the slow movement, the vocal manner provided a perfect

Example 14 (a) *Arsilda, regina di Ponto* (opera, RV 700), Act I scene 15;
(b) *Nel partir da te, mio caro* (cantata, RV 661), final aria

Example 15 *The Hunt* (No. 10), II, with notional text-setting

environment for improvisation: a natural simplicity, and a melodic guise that
is familiar to the soloist because it is common to many composers' vocal pieces.
Doubtless Vivaldi also valued the concerto's slow movement as an additional
outlet for tender *arie patetiche* and thereby as the means of creating meaningful
contrasts to his fast movements.

Hundreds of lines in aria texts – whether set by Vivaldi or not – would match
phrases of *The Hunt* provided that they scan suitably when the normal practice
of synaloepha (the coalescence of adjacent vowels) is observed. In Example 15,
as an experiment, lines selected from Vivaldi's first opera (*Ottone in villa*,
1713) are set to the opening phrases. The first line would have to begin with
a stressed syllable ('*Mi*sero'), the second with an unstressed one. The first
must be a *verso piano* (a 'soft' line ending strong–weak), while the second
might be a *verso sdrucciolo* – a 'sliding' line ending strong–weak–weak
(the proparoxytone accent) as in 'a*ma*bile' – or another *verso piano*. Finally,
a *verso tronco* ('truncated' line) is required – ending, that is, with an accent
('tradi*tor*').

To improve upon this nonsensical textual collage one would have to find a
single aria text that is not only suitable in terms of its metre, number of lines

Example 16   Tartini, Concerto in C (D12), alternative slow movement

and syllabic patterns but also evocative of an appropriate affection. But that is beside the point: one is not suggesting that Vivaldi composed the movement by setting an actual aria line by line only to omit the words. The music consists of the stylized language of word-setting not real word-setting, though it is possible that some suddenly remembered lines, in triggering an association in the composer's mind between sound and meaning, were the stimulus for this mode of composition.

Similar one-bar phrases are legion among Vivaldi's slow common-time pieces elsewhere, especially in sonatas. We find them throughout the central movements of *Winter*, No. 9 and No. 11, but in combination with extended phrases, sustained notes and wide melodic leaps – features idiomatic more to instrumental playing than to singing. Evidently, the influence of text-setting tended to recede as Vivaldi warmed to his task. Some movements – the Largo of *The Cuckoo* RV 335, for instance – have very elaborate solo figures that cause the sense of the location of notional syllables to be lost; little more than one-bar phrasing remains as a trace of the style's origin.

Such pieces, if they are not purely abstract inventions, must be very close in principle to many movements, both slow and fast, in Giuseppe Tartini's violin concertos of the 1730s and beyond, that possess a more tangible semantic and phonic connection with literary texts. Tartini would quote, often in a simple code, a line or several lines of an aria text – mostly from Metastasio's dramas – as a caption to a movement. Minos Dounias, who deciphered the code, regards these captions as 'mottoes' that inspired Tartini's themes;[7] Paul Brainard observes that their 'pathetic-dramatic cast is often strangely appropriate to that of Tartini's effusive musical language'.[8] It would appear, indeed, that the solo part's melodic phrasing was sometimes derived from the prosodic rhythm of the text in question – at least as much as the style and general mood of the music were influenced by the text's meaning. In the case of the second (alternative) slow movement of the violin concerto D12, it is possible to match the first quatrain of the indicated aria (from Metastasio's *Demofoonte*, 1733) to Tartini's opening bars: Example 16.[9]

Whether Vivaldi consciously fostered the slow movement as a 'song without words' to this extent will remain a matter for conjecture. The significance of the word 'Aria', with which the composer labelled the common-time Andante of the violin concerto RV 336, is difficult to assess when it is the only surviving verbal clue. Nevertheless, the demonstrable aria-like expression in *Winter* and many other examples speaks for itself.

6

The Four Seasons

It is ironic that *The Four Seasons*, some of the best-known music of all time, remain an enigma. Several interrelated questions need to be answered before a reasonably complete view of Vivaldi's actions can ever be reached. When were the sonnets written, and by whom? Was the music based on the poetry or vice versa? Were the programme's ideas Vivaldi's own? Why were extra explanatory captions added for the works' publication in Op. 8? Such uncertainties leave us blinkered when it comes to appraising the music – and the concertos themselves, far from providing answers, serve to confuse us all the more. Taken at face value, the works seem individualized, concerned only with their own narratives. Their collective integrity exists nonetheless, residing to some extent in intertextual relationships but principally in Vivaldi's approach to different seasonal pictures: a consistency of method, through which distinct ideas are shown to be complementary.

Musical principles

One cannot say, as Beethoven said of the 'Pastoral' Symphony, that the *Seasons* are 'more the expression of feeling than painting'. Nevertheless, Vivaldi manages to maintain feeling while indulging in vivid painting. We observed in Chapters 3–5 how his movements function – even without the prop of a programme – in at least two dimensions: a foreground in which 'events' and musical vocabulary strike the imagination, and a background forged from key, metre, tempo and figurative relationships that places the foreground in some kind of context, whether tangibly meaningful or not. The fast movements also possess an essential third dimension: a structure that can unfold like a dramatic plot and even be transmuted somewhere along its course. In short, the composer's customary method of the mid- to late 1710s encompassed all the factors one might associate with programme composition. Arguably, the *Seasons*' only difference is that an external programme caused his method to be more focused than usual.

Since the *Seasons* are solo concertos that retain the genre's essential technical principles, their conception cannot have been devoted exclusively to the programmatic function. Their excellence is a measure of how successfully Vivaldi compromised in two directions, adapting both structure and the soloist's contribution to the programme and very probably tinkering with the programme to make sure that it fitted standard movement-types and the demands of solo virtuosity. These works, indeed, are almost as highly regarded for their remarkable technical feats – the *bariolage* in *Summer* (III, bars 51–4/247–50), for instance – as for their imagery and narrative.[1] Slow movements, being short and lacking episodic change, are treated in the *Seasons* as tableaux: each a static scene painted with considerable textural depth. Fast movements, however, offered more scope. The needs of the solo concerto dictated that the programme must include many transient events, or sounds that do not last long (bird-song, thunder, etc.), suitable for foreground-painting in episodes. While the solo violin part is an ideal medium for pictorialism and onomatopoeia, Vivaldi did not hesitate to orchestrate an episode more fully if this was warranted by the force or plurality of the subject depicted.

The *Seasons*' background 'feeling' or emotional weight is immensely strong, carried by several musical factors in combination: the 'world' of the tonic key; ritornellos that represent a scene's unchanging aspect; and a tonal-periodic procedure that encourages the listener to sense a movement's direction despite change in the foreground. All the principles observed in Chapter 3 apply, but they are stretched to their limits by the needs of the programme. Thus we find ritornellos with peculiarities, modulation hastened or delayed unexpectedly, and more motivic relationships than are customary. An impression of the *Seasons*' structural complexity may be gained by comparing their fast-movement schemes shown in Example 17 with those of Op. 8 Nos. 5–12. (See Example 6; the diagrammatic manner is explained on p. 40.) The procedure we have called 'progressive ritornello form' (pp. 38–9) is manifest in several instances; in the first movement of *Summer*, its logic demands the substitution of the whole ritornello. These and other points are clarified towards the end of this chapter, where the concertos are assessed individually.

There is much evidence of significant key-associations in relation to the cycle's programme, not least in respect of the concertos' tonic keys. The choice of F major for *Autumn* is easy to understand; being the natural key of *corni da caccia*, it was traditionally associated with hunting and bucolic settings. An implication of anxiety and threat in G minor, for *Summer*, has already been observed (pp. 45 and 58–9). E major and F minor are rarely found as tonic keys among Vivaldi's instrumental works, though his occasional use of them

Example 17   Tonal schemes: fast movements of *The Four Seasons*

in opera makes their meaning clear.[2] The former, perfect for *Spring*, is variously associated with brilliant light, pleasant rest (as in the concerto *Il riposo* RV 270) and amorousness (*L'amoroso* RV 271). F minor, elsewhere having the unpleasant connotations of horror, vengeance and extreme grief, is entirely apt as the chilling backdrop for *Winter*.

The programme

The seasons of the year are a wonderfully evocative theme to which artists throughout history have responded in different ways. But for good literary products one had best look elsewhere. The *Seasons*' anonymous sonnets are clumsy, amateurish verse of little merit: they disappoint because we expect sonnets to be polished jewels. Their weakness, in itself, is unimportant, but it raises the possibility that Vivaldi was their author. They show elements of the Venetian dialect – 'mossoni' instead of 'mosconi', for instance – and Venetian spellings (e. g., 'canni' for *cani*) of the kind that appear in Vivaldi's autograph letters.[3] The composer is known on occasion to have rewritten aria and recitative texts and may well have had sufficient skill to write poetry unaided.

In the original edition of Op. 8, the four texts, each called *sonnetto dimostrativo* ('illustrative sonnet'), are presented all together in the principal violin partbook.[4] They are transcribed here with their cue-letters that direct the reader to particular passages in the music; we have added horizontal lines to show how each text corresponds in portions to the three movements of its respective concerto. The present translations are precisely literal ones; English versions that are more artistically satisfying – but typically less accurate – may be found in the notes accompanying many recordings.

The merit of the sonnets lies in what they imply rather than how they imply it, but they fail (as do the added captions) to express the *Seasons*' general themes coherently. The only way to bring the actual programme and its subtle cross-references into sharp focus is to take Vivaldi's musical treatment into account as well.

The whole cycle is concerned with humankind's relationship with nature, and thus we encounter significant thematic similarities and balancing contrasts. Nature is regarded as benign in *Spring* and *Autumn* and malign in *Summer* and *Winter*. This results in nature-centred idealism for spring and autumn, as opposed to more realistic, people-centred views of summer and winter. Mythological allusions abound, but they are at their strongest when Spring is personified in an Arcadian scene with nymphs and shepherds.

Autumn is less static and softened with human touches, but its references to Bacchus and hunters show that it too owes something to the pastoral tradition. *Spring* and *Autumn* are united in celebration: first of Nature herself and then of her bounty.

In *Summer* and *Winter*, the mythological names for winds are diminished to mere tokens by an overwhelming and distinctly psychological concentration on man's perils and joys. As with spring and autumn, the summer–winter axis has its own equilibrium. Both *Summer* and *Winter* are concerned with discomfort and danger, but the former is dominated by one man's vulnerability, the latter with people's enjoyment against the odds. If *Summer* is the emotional fulcrum of the whole cycle, *Winter* is the weight that tips the balance. *Winter*, indeed, has the most idiosyncratic sonnet; significantly perhaps, it gives twelve cues to musical illustration (letters A–N), not the seven or eight of the others. Standing apart from the traditional pretence of bucolic pleasures (or obverse perils), it draws us positively into a modern urban world of the early eighteenth century in which malign Nature can be overcome. Here at last one senses that the sonneteer writes from personal experience; it is worth noting, in this regard, that Venice's lagoon froze over in the severe winter of 1708–9. By the end of the cycle, we have come a long way from the detached, stylized view of spring.

The programme's sophistication makes the sonnets' inefficiency seem all the more significant. It is especially intriguing that the poems' repetitive tendency, in itself poor, reflects something worthy in the music. It seems excessive, for instance, for sleep to be invoked four times in three sonnets, and yet the music, conveying such distinct senses of sleep, justifies it. Much of the success of the concertos as a unified set relies, indeed, on presenting the same attribute (warmth, winds, bird-song, thunder, etc.) in different lights so that parallels are drawn between contrasting emotional results. The works' several intertextual relationships are devoted to that purpose. Consider, for instance, the Sirocco wind in the finale of *Winter* (from bar 101/182), designed as a cyclic back-reference to the opening of *Summer*; or the dotted-rhythm accompaniments in the slow movements of *Spring* and *Summer* – welcome and unwelcome murmurings, respectively; or the uniformity of melodic contour and comparable harmony that connects the celebratory initial ritornellos of *Spring* and *Autumn*. Vivaldi's leitmotif of four descending notes (see pp. 54–5) recurs strategically to link *Spring* with *Summer*, as we shall see, and appears also in *Autumn* and *Winter*. Various three-note contractions and chromatic transformations help further to cement the set together.

Making better sense in the music than in the poems, the cycle's thematic

La primavera

A   Giunt'è la Primavera e festosetti
B   La salutan gl'Augei con lieto canto,
C   E i fonti allo spirar de' Zeffiretti
       Con dolce mormorio scorrono intanto:

D   Vengon' coprendo l'aer di nero amanto
       E Lampi, e tuoni ad annuntiarla eletti
E   Indi tacendo questi, gl'Augelletti;
       Tornan' di nuovo al lor canoro incanto:

F   E quindi sul fiorito ameno prato
       Al caro mormorio di fronde e piante
       Dorme 'l Caprar col fido can' à lato.

G   Di pastoral Zampogna al suon festante
       Danzan Ninfe e Pastor nel tetto amato
       Di primavera all'apparir brillante.

L'estade

A   Sotto dura staggion dal sole accesa
       Langue l'huom, langue 'l gregge, ed arde il Pino;
B   Scioglie il Cucco la Voce, e tosto intesa
C   Canta la Tortorella e 'l gardelino.

D   Zeffiro dolce spira, mà contesa
       Muove Borea improviso al suo vicino;
E   E piange il Pastorel, perche sospesa
       Teme fiera borasca, e 'l suo destino;

F   Toglie alle membra lasse il suo riposo
       Il timore de' Lampi, e tuoni fieri
       E de mosche, e mossoni il stuol furioso!

G   Ah che pur troppo i suoi timor son veri
       Tuona e fulmina il Ciel e grandinoso
       Tronca il capo alle spiche e a' grani alteri.

Spring

[A]   Spring has arrived and merrily
[B]   the birds hail her with happy song
[C]   and, meanwhile, at the breath of the Zephyrs,
        the streams flow with a sweet murmur:

[D]   thunder and lightning, chosen to proclaim her,
        come covering the sky with a black mantle,
[E]   and then, when these fall silent, the little birds
        return once more to their melodious incantation:

[F]   and so, on the pleasant, flowery meadow,
        to the welcome murmuring of fronds and trees,
        the goatherd sleeps with his trusty dog beside him.

[G]   To the festive sound of a shepherd's bagpipe,
        nymphs and shepherds dance beneath the beloved roof
        at the joyful appearance of spring.

Summer

[A]   Beneath the harsh season inflamed by the sun,
        Man languishes, the flock languishes, and the pine tree burns;
[B]   the cuckoo unleashes its voice and, as soon as it is heard,
[C]   the turtle dove sings and the goldfinch too.

[D]   Sweet Zephyrus blows, but Boreas suddenly
        opens a dispute with his neighbour;
[E]   and the shepherd weeps, for he fears
        a fierce storm looming – and his destiny;

[F]   the fear of lightning and fierce thunder
        and the furious swarm of flies and blowflies
        deprives his weary limbs of repose.

[G]   Oh alas! his fears are only too true.
        The sky thunders, flares, and with hailstones
        severs the heads of the proud grain crops.

L'autunno

A Celebra il Vilanel con balli e Canti
  Del felice raccolto il bel piacere
B E del liquor di Bacco accesi tanti
C Finiscono col sonno il lor godere

D Fà ch' ogn'uno tralasci e balli e canti
  L'aria che temperata dà piacere,
  E la Staggion ch'invita tanti e tanti
  D'un dolcissimo sonno al bel godere.

E I cacciator alla nov'alba à caccia
  Con corni, schioppi, e canni escono fuore
F Fugge la belva, e seguono la traccia;

G Già sbigottita, e lassa al gran rumore
  De' schioppi e canni, ferita minaccia
H Languida di fuggir, mà oppressa muore.

L'inverno

A Aggiacciato tremar trà nevi algenti
B Al severo spirar d'orrido Vento,
C Correr battendo i piedi ogni momento;
D E pel soverchio gel batter i denti;

E Passar al foco i di quieti e contenti
  Mentre la pioggia fuor bagna ben cento

F Caminar sopra 'l giaccio, e à passo lento
G Per timor di cader gersene intenti;

H Gir forte[,] sdruzziolar, cader à terra
I Di nuovo ir sopra 'l giaccio e correr forte
L Sin ch' il giaccio si rompe, e si disserra;

M Sentir uscir dalle ferrate porte
N Sirocco[,] Borea, e tutti i Venti in guerra
  Quest'è 'l verno, mà tal, che gioia apporte.

Autumn

[A]   The peasant celebrates in dance and song
        the sweet pleasure of the rich harvest
[B]   and, fired by Bacchus' liquor,
[C]   many end their enjoyment in slumber.

———

[D]   The air, which, fresher now, lends contentment,
        and the season which invites so many
        to the great pleasure of sweetest slumber,
        make each one abandon dance and song.

———

[E]   At the new dawn the hunters set out on the hunt
        with horns, guns and dogs.
[F]   The wild beast flees, and they follow its track;

[G]   already bewildered, and wearied by the great noise
        of the guns and dogs, wounded,
[H]   it threatens weakly to escape, but, overwhelmed, dies.

Winter

[A]   To shiver, frozen, amid icy snows,
[B]   at the harsh wind's chill breath;
[C]   to run, stamping one's feet at every moment;
[D]   with one's teeth chattering on account of the excessive cold;

———

[E]   to pass the days of calm and contentment by the fireside
        while the rain outside drenches a hundred others;

———

[F]   to walk on the ice, and with slow steps
[G]   to move about cautiously for fear of falling;

[H]   to go fast, slip, fall to the ground;
[I]   to go on the ice again and run fast
[L]   until the ice cracks and breaks open;

[M]   to hear, as they sally forth through the iron-clad gates,
[N]   Sirocco, Boreas, and all the winds at war.
        This is winter, but of a kind to bring joy.

Table 4

Work	Mvt.	Bar	Part(s)	Caption	Translation
Spring	II	1	viola	*Il cane che grida*	the dog that barks
Summer	I	1	all parts	*Languidezza per il caldo*	languor due to the heat
	I	78	violins	*Zeffiretti dolci spira*	sweet Zephyrs blow
	I	90	viola	*Venti impettuosi*	impetuous winds
	I	90	*basso*	*Venti diversi*	various winds
	I	116	solo violin	*Il pianto del villanello*	the countryman's lament
Autumn	I	32	solo violin	*L'ubriaco*	the inebriate
	I	41	non-solo parts	*Ubriachi*	inebriates
	I	67	solo violin	*Ubriaco*	the inebriate
	I	89	solo violin	*L'ubriaco che dorme*	the inebriate who sleeps
	II	1	all except solo	*Ubriachi dormienti*	sleeping inebriates
Winter	I	33	*basso*	*Venti*	winds

threads hint, crucially, that the programme to which Vivaldi worked was originally independent of the sonnets. Could it be that the music was at least planned – perhaps even completed – before the idea of illustrative sonnets was ever entertained? Most commentators, including the present writer,[5] have dismissed that view; the many correspondences between verbal description and musical depiction are so close that it seemed almost inconceivable that the concertos could have been composed without reference to the sonnets. However, the billing of the sonnets both in the 1725 edition and the Manchester manuscripts is categorical – in all cases, the poem is described as *sopra* (based on) the concerto in question – and challenges us to imagine a scenario along the following lines. Vivaldi first decides on the ideas of the programme and begins to compose the music accordingly. Sooner or later, he realizes that the music by itself cannot convey its meaning to the listener. Sonnets are the chosen solution, and he or a collaborator cobbles them together. It is a botched job that suffices for most purposes (as the Manchester manuscripts reveal). But for the *Seasons'* publication in Op. 8, Vivaldi feels the need to explain the music more accurately with captions.

Most of the captions merely repeat or paraphrase words contained in the sonnets while usefully pinpointing their context, sometimes a particular part or a bar other than the location of a cue-letter (see Plate 1). But a few, listed in Table 4, clarify some aspects of the programme that the sonnets fail to convey. We discover that much of the first movement in *Autumn* concerns the antics of one particular drunkard ('L'ubriaco'), whereas the sonnet refers simply to 'many' having been 'fired by Bacchus' liquor'. Vivaldi was presumably inventive enough to conceive this and the rest of the *Seasons*' themes for himself, but the programme's sophistication hints that the sequence and substance of the ideas were drawn from literature of a better pedigree than the sonnets.

The English connection

The key that begins to reveal the *Seasons*' innermost secrets is the pair of complementary poems by John Milton that explores the cheerful and pensive sides to the human character: *L'allegro* and *Il penseroso*, written in *c*. 1631–2 and familiar to us from Handel's setting (1740). The essence of the *Seasons*' programme appears to have originated – almost certainly indirectly – from Milton's work. To the best of my knowledge, this remarkable correlation has not hitherto been recognized.

The *Seasons* represent only a small minority of the themes and allusions contained in *L'allegro* and *Il penseroso* (which together run to over 300 lines) – but largely in Milton's order. The closest concurrences are detailed in Table 5. *Spring* relates to the passage early in *L'allegro* (lines 11–40) that invokes the goddess who can bring pleasures. *L'allegro* then dwells on the pleasures of country-living (lines 41–116), including some associated with summer that are absent in the *Seasons*. Strong correspondence, this time with *Autumn*, next occurs when harvest-time pleasures are evoked: dancing after the crops are gathered, drinking, story-telling and contented sleep. One has only to search back to lines 53–4 to find reference to a hunt. We note in particular that *L'allegro* contains an apparent precedent, in the form of a story about weary Hobgoblin (Puck), for the 'Ubriaco' episode that, as we saw earlier, is missing from the sonnet.

A model for *Summer* appears obliquely, but just as tangibly, in *Il penseroso*. The poet, alone, is deep in the pleasures of contemplation; though his thoughts induce melancholy, they are not particularly disturbing. *Summer* picks up on isolated ideas, retaining some intact (the solitude of the man; the desire to hear the nightingale in May; disturbed sleep) but turning the rest on its head.

Table 5

	The Four Seasons	Milton, *L'allegro* (A) and *Il penseroso* (P)
Spring, I	Spring is proclaimed	Euphrosyne (Blitheness) is invoked (A, 11–12)[a]
	attendant Zephyrs	*The frolic wind that breathes the spring Zephyr, with Aurora playing* (A, 18–19)[b]
Spring, II	pleasant flowers, murmuring of fronds and trees	*There on beds of violets blue And fresh-blown roses wash'd in dew* (A, 21–2)
Spring, III	festive dancing	*Come and trip it as you go On the light fantastic toe* (A, 33–4)
Summer, I	stillness, apprehension, waiting for the nightingale	*And the mute Silence hist along, 'Less Philomel will deign a song* (P, 55–6)[c]
	plaintive bird-songs	*Sweet bird, that shunn'st the noise of folly, Most musical, most melancholy!* (P, 61–2)
	fierce winds	*While rocking winds are piping loud, Or usher'd with a shower still When the gust hath blown his fill* (P, 125–8)
Summer, II	sounds of insects	*While the bee with honey'd thigh, That at her flowery work doth sing* (P, 142–3)
	troubled sleep	*Entice the dewy-feather'd sleep; And let some strange mysterious dream Wave at his wings . . .* (P, 146–8)
Summer, III	after sleep: the storm sent by forces ill-disposed to man	after sleep: sweet music sent by forces well-disposed to man (P, 151–4)[d]
Autumn, I	harvest-time dancing	*To many a youth and many a maid Dancing in the chequer'd shade* (A, 95–6)[e]
	drinking	*Then to the spicy nut-brown ale* (A, 100)
	one peasant's drunken antics and final collapse	tale of Hobgoblin, well-known for pranks, who finally stretches out at the fireside (A, 105–12)[f]

Table 5 *(cont.)*

	The Four Seasons	Milton, *L'allegro* (A) and *Il penseroso* (P)
Autumn, II	sleep in pleasant air	*Thus done the tales, to bed they creep,* *By whispering winds soon lulled asleep* (A, 115–16)
Autumn, III	hunting at dawn;	*Oft listening how the hounds and horn* *Cheerly rouse the slumbering morn* (A, 53–4)

Notes to Table 5:

a   Euphrosyne is one of the Graces and a goddess of festivity.

b   Zephyr (the west wind) is the son of Aeolus (god of the winds) and Aurora (bright dawn), and the lover of Flora (goddess of flowers).

c   The fate of Philomel had been to be changed into a nightingale.

d   'And as I awake, sweet music breath / Above, about or underneath, / Sent by some spirit to mortals good / Or the unseen Genius of the wood.'

e   It is clear, from lines 87–90, that this refers to holiday revels at harvest-time.

f   Lines 110–12: 'Then lies him down the lubber fiend, / And stretch'd out all the chimney's length, / Basks at the fire his hairy strength'.

According to the old superstition implicit in Milton's words,[6] one is doomed to failure in love unless one hears the nightingale before the cuckoo – the point of departure for *Summer*, which fatally has the cuckoo first. Thereafter, Milton's harmless winds and honeyed bee become malevolent things. The outcome in *Summer* – the destructive storm that fills the sky – is a bitter parody of Milton's sweet music that brings 'all Heaven before mine eyes' (line 166).

Or so it seems. The relationship is strong, but it is of course unlikely that Vivaldi had access to Milton's poems in their original form – and still less likely that he knew English. It is perfectly possible, however, that he came by the ideas from another source. Milton had visited Italy on his tour of Europe in 1638–9, and, through contacts, his work doubtless became disseminated there. He was fluent in Italian and greatly admired the language as a medium for poetry; if he did not translate *L'allegro* and *Il penseroso* himself, he may have encouraged an Italian colleague to do so. Various derivatives might have been in circulation by the 1710s although Milton bibliographies list no published translations of the two poems into Italian (or, for that matter, into French or Latin) that antedate *The Four Seasons*. The source of Vivaldi's ideas might conceivably have been some literature that drew on Milton in an unacknowledged way. Until the intermediate link is discovered, the Milton–Vivaldi connection remains at the level of hypothesis.[7] In particular, we cannot be sure of the extent to which the *Seasons*' sonnets and added captions possess an indirect linguistic derivation from Milton as well as a thematic one. That is an important issue, especially regarding *Winter*.

Milton makes no reference to winter – a fact that is a clue to why the themes of *Winter* are distinctly more bourgeois and less traditional than those of the other three works. Rather like Charles Jennens's *Il moderato* appended to Milton's poems for Handel's setting, the programme for *Winter*, as we noted above, is a modern concept that serves to reconcile the cycle's seventeenth-century aesthetic to the philosophical stance of the eighteenth century. Its inspiration, however, appears to stem from Milton. Immediately after its allusions to autumn, *L'allegro* turns to pleasures of town life (lines 117–34): pageants, tournaments and masques that produce 'the busy hum of men'. Sport and fun are the equivalent in *Winter*. The sonnet's celebration of skating, with winds breaking free, employs vocabulary deeply redolent of Milton's lines 139–44:

> In notes with many a winding bout
> Of linkèd sweetness long drawn out,
> With wanton heed and giddy cunning
> The melting voice through mazes running,
> Untwisting all the chains that tie
> The hidden soul of harmony.

Here (as in *Il penseroso*) Milton is praising good music: its 'hidden soul' is released when it is composed with both 'wanton heed' (capricious attention) and 'giddy cunning' (skill guided by whim). Could not these oxymorons be the distant origin of 'the trial of harmony and invention', and skating-on-ice a metaphor for Vivaldi's daring art?

Spring's raptures

The cycle's brightest, most optimistic music is heard first, as befits the season. It is also the most formal: a ritornello with the heaviness and poise of a courtly dance, suited to the proclaiming of a goddess. Vivaldi adapted the ritornello for the opera *Giustino* (RV 717, 1724) as a short *sinfonia*, also in E major, during which the goddess Fortune appears in a brightly lit scene.[8] We hear immediately an aspiration to the note b^2 in bar 1 and throughout the ritornello, and solos that begin on the fifth of the chord (bars 14 and 59). These open sounds of exposed fifths seem to reach high to the deity in 'the beloved roof'; the same rationale might also explain why the bolts of lightning in bar 45 flash

Example 18   *Arsilda, regina di Ponto* RV 700 (1716),
aria 'Quel usignolo' (Act II scene 9)

up – also to b^2 – not down.[9] The stormy passage, for which the first modulation
has been reserved, presents no great sense of conflict. It might have been
worked in simply to add a transitory event to an otherwise static scene and
to provoke some volatility at the movement's centre. Nevertheless, the birds'
feathers are somewhat ruffled as a result (bars 59–65), as if to show that Nature
will not remain faithful. In opera, Vivaldi had employed the same combination
of tiered nightingale-calls and rising chromaticism – innocent cheerfulness
and uneasy wistfulness – when addressing infidelity in love: Example 18.

In the slow movement, the gentle rustling of plants recalls the figure that
evoked the wind-lapped streams (first movement, from bar 31): the key word
in the sonnet, for both contexts, is 'mormorio' (murmuring). Now in C# minor,
the music has the zest of immense freshness and perhaps a hint of the
wistfulness that crept in earlier. Hushed violins (when played well) can truly
achieve that eeriness one senses when trees in bloom are swept by breezes.
The dog's barks are articulated *sempre molto forte e strappato* (very loud and
with 'wrenched' bowing throughout) – not because they must be loud in an
absolute sense (for how could the goatherd sleep?) but because the viola player
alone provides a percussive bass.

More festive celebration follows, this time in rustic compound metre and

Example 19 *Spring*, III (a) bars 10–11; (b) bars 25–6; (c) bar 76

with drones associated with bagpipes. Aptly for a *Danza pastorale*, the movement has a rondo-like structure, reverting to the tonic key for a central passage (bars 40–53/162–75) well before the end-play is expected, and imposing it abruptly in bar 58/180 immediately after a cadence in the dominant. The last effect is particularly reminiscent of the corresponding context in the rondo-finale of Bach's violin concerto in E major.

According to the sonnet, the finale concerns nothing but dancing. However, Vivaldi employs a structural 'plot' of the kind examined in Chapter 3, where tonic-minor pathos enhances the end-play. Musical 'events' occur in rapid succession from bar 61/183 – the sudden introduction of E minor, a modal shift to D major, a new sequence and then plaintive chromaticism – and of course they do not necessarily mean anything. But one wonders if such a disruptive passage is not intended to remind us that happiness can never be entirely carefree. In this connection we notice the appearance of the four-note descent. Absent from the first two movements, it is conspicuous throughout the finale in various guises: Example 19 gives a selection. The motif will occur equally prominently in *Summer*, seemingly as a symbol of disaster. If Vivaldi hoped that it would have that sinister implication, he may well have reasoned that it must first insinuate itself as part of spring's innocence.

Summer's ruin

Vivaldi's vision of the fear and destruction associated with a *temporale* – a violent storm, brewed by the warm winds from the Sahara, of a kind that regularly afflicts Italy in summer – is arguably his most inspired characterized concerto. Of all the *Seasons*, only *Summer* has a relentless progression across its three movements from anticipation to realization of a single event, and this is reflected in the fast movements' unusually high degree of motivic integration. Vivaldi's four-note leitmotif not only makes the connection between the violence of the storm (finale, bars 1–4, g^1–f^1–$e\flat^1$–d^1, comparably in bars 6–9, 21–8 and 70–3) and, in diminution, its cutting effects (solo part, bars 41–8 and 109–13). With perfect logic, it also characterizes the winds that threaten to bring the storm: d^3–c^3–$b\flat^2$–a^2 in bars 94–101 of the first movement (similarly from bar 155). Descent through the tetrachord in a minor key is a melodic feature common to many composers' works – frequently those concerning suffering.[10] Haydn's use of it, for the opening bars of 'The Seasons' (1801), is particularly close to Vivaldi's: played harshly in G minor, it conveys Winter's undiminished threat with similar menace.

Other relationships, too, compel us to consider the movements of *Summer* collectively. All three are set in G minor, with all that that implies for the continuity of the fear-and-realization theme. All possess rapid figurations of similar type for the whole band, in turn representing winds, thunder and the storm itself. Both fast movements are in triple metre – thus in apposition as cause and effect – and solo passages are at a premium in both since nothing less than *tutti* scoring can achieve the force attributed to Nature in this instance.

The finale's unprecedented representation of destructive power is made all the more effective by what precedes it: an immense tightening of tension throughout the first movement that the weary lyricism of the slow movement cannot dissipate. Many of the first movement's peculiarities deserve attention. First we hear a ritornello that is anything but typical: a set of disarmingly 'slow' gestures, metrically dislocated, that must represent the lethargy of the anxious man at least as much as the oppressive heat of an airless day. Here Vivaldi introduces wilting figures that will remain significant: falling quavers, often with the jarring sound of the augmented second, and, embedded in the cadential element, the four-note descent transformed by Neapolitan-sixth harmony: Example 20a. The cuckoo's voice, itself a premonition of disaster, and the other bird-songs do nothing to relieve the uncomfortable sense of expectancy. Fixed in G minor and recalling the four-note motif (bass, bars 63–6), they intensify – even to deafening proportions (bars 49–52) – the man's awareness of danger. Modulation, long-delayed, happens only when the 'sweet zephyrs' disturb the stillness. The descent to D minor occurs over eight innocent-sounding bars – Example 20b (each bar represented by one crotchet) – in a fateful melodic contour (*y*) that relates back to the ritornello and forward, as we shall see, to the man's utter distress. The irony is clear: breezes that in other circumstances bring welcome refreshment are the harbinger of destruction. Although it is *tutti*, the subsequent battle of winds (from bar 90) continues the episode, prior to the ritornello at bar 110. But the same music, when recalled in G minor from bar 155, functions as a substitute ritornello in this special example of 'progressive ritornello form': what might have been merely a transient, inconsequential feature of the weather proves to be a lasting and ultimately damaging one.

Example 20   *Summer*, I (a) bars 21–5; (b) bars 82–9 (reduction)

That realization dawns earlier, when the movement's volatility, end-play and cadenza fuse together in one of Baroque music's most radical creations: 'Il pianto del villanello' (the countryman's lament), bars 116–54. The person represented is not the 'shepherd boy' that many translators have made of the sonnet's 'il pastorel' – for why should a mere boy be so distraught? The diminutive form of *pastore* (like that of *villano*) was surely preferred as a term of endearment and perhaps because the line in the sonnet scanned better as a result. He is a man with whom we have sympathy because his precarious livelihood – his crops soon to be ruined – hangs in the balance.

Examples 21a and 21b show the derivation of the episode's fundamental ascending and descending cells, *x* and *y*, first heard in elaborated form in bars 116 and 117 which are themselves based on the melodic shape of the preceding ritornello (bars 110–15). Though we hear it as improvisatory, all variation throughout the whole lament rests on *x* and *y*; even when not being played, the cells remain implicitly in the harmonic progression (in bars 126–31, for instance). Example 21c clarifies this in reduction, giving the structure of the music's tortuous transition to the point where G minor is restored (keys are noted beneath the staves). The first three staves, in alignment, show chromatic descent in three comparable passes, each beginning with an upward leap in the bass – in two instances a tritone (*z*). Most remarkable is the enharmonic change in bars 122–3 that gains tonal 'height' in preparation for the second pass, more anguished than the first. Chromatic progress is broken in bar 136 when the music settles briefly under the influence of sequential harmony (*w*): the man's sheer panic comes under control as sorrow. Now the bass too acquires motivic significance, providing two versions of *y* in augmentation as the route to G minor. Above, the violin part also incorporates the long form of *y* and its inversion reached through tritone *z*.

In the cadenza (bars 144–54) with which the lament concludes, motif *y* repeatedly strikes to the heart over a subdominant pedal, with Neapolitan-sixth harmony that was prefigured in bar 139 and as early as the first ritornello. A better way of forcing us to feel the man's loneliness and vulnerability can scarcely be imagined.

Example 21   *Summer*, I, bars 116–44

Autumn's revels

Struggle with Nature, so central to *Summer*, is a theme absent from *Autumn*. Having achieved a temporary victory by harnessing Nature's power, man may now enjoy the spoils (crops, ale, wild animals to be killed) in untroubled leisure. Selfish indulgence is hinted at both in the sonnet – which eschews the idea, present in *Spring*, that Nature ought gratefully to be honoured – and in music that concentrates on carousal and sport. Only the quarry experiences struggle, but the single phrase devoted to its distress and pain (Example 22) is mere tokenism – albeit nicely timed for the cadenza – in Vivaldi's picture of the pursuit of pleasure. It is no coincidence that *Autumn* elicits from the soloist the *Seasons*' most sustained displays of extrovert virtuosity, for in this

Example 22   *Autumn*, III, bars 136–41

way man's brash confidence is superimposed on our perception of depicted events.

The first movement manages to convey crudeness with artful grace, initially in a repetitive ritornello of 'primitive' harmony and a similar first solo rooted to the steps of the peasants' dance. Thereafter, Vivaldi's structural game-plan – increasing musical volatility to reflect increasing inebriation – is more subtle than it might at first sight appear. Timed with the drunkard's first serious totter (bar 41), the first change of key is not the normal step to the dominant but the beginning of a radical modulation – to G minor, with its overtones of impending disaster. The movement's second phase thus arrives early as if the sudden onset of drunkenness comes as a shock to both inebriate and bystander. Already dangerously wayward, the music's behaviour now takes on a drunk's capacity for self-delusion: an assured (but premature) return to the tonic key in bars 72–4, followed by a convincing lunge (in the wrong place) to the dominant. From there, the penultimate ritornello restores F major in a welter of new syncopation as the dance dissolves into an unreal, spinning world. With the sound of merry-making retreating to the background (violin parts, bars 97–105), the wretched man's stupor finally induces sleep.

While the sonnet would have us believe that the season's fresh air gently 'invites' the peasants to sweet slumber, the slow movement's caption 'Ubriachi dormienti' (sleeping drunks) leaves us in no doubt of the true cause. This slumber, after all, is not so very sweet. With frequent dissonance, unpredictable phrasing and extreme tonal dislocation, the Adagio seems rather to represent the fits and starts of confused dreams, and was appropriately reused later in a ghostly context as the movement called 'Il sonno' (Sleep) in two versions of *La notte* (RV 104 and 439).[11] Like the motif in *Summer* identified as *y* (see Examples 20b and 21), the principal figure evokes an uneasy, troubled sense: Example 23a. An association between sleep and terrors is implicit, indeed, in the figure's recurrence in 'Sonno, se pur sei sonno e non orrore' sung by the imprisoned Manlius at the beginning of Act III of *Tito Manlio* RV 738 (1719): Example 23b.[12] Even the rare direction 'Il cembalo arpeggio' might indicate that the drunks are in need of relief; in Act I scene 10 of *Dorilla*

Example 23   (a) *Autumn*, II, bars 6–8;
(b) *Tito Manlio*, 'Sonno, se pur sei sonno', bars 2–4

in *Tempe* RV 709, harpsichord arpeggiation is similarly called for when Dorilla begs the gods for pity.

The finale, subtitled 'La caccia', is a *tour de force* that perfectly reflects a vigorous outdoor romp. Possessing the common denominator of progressive animation though its episodes, it complements the first movement through parody to some extent. The peasants' crudeness translates into the presumably genteel skill of the hunters, the antics and danger of the drunk into those of the quarry. Even the first solo resembles that of the earlier movement in its formality and harmonic style, with double-stopped figures derived from the ritornello. As is customary in a movement's central phase, the band contributes important phrases of articulation in the form of bursts of gunfire (bars 82–6/242–6 and 92–6/252–6) – in demisemiquavers that signal both the musical climax and the animal's demise.

Winter's reconciliation

In *Winter*, Nature is at her most terrifying in the bleakest of environments. This is evident in the tuneless opening ritornello, with cruel dissonance and icy articulation, and the fury of the wind that follows. It is certainly a vision of horror to Vivaldi's way of thinking. He would later set an aria about blood chilling at the sight of a ghost – 'Gelido in ogni vena' ('Icy in every vein')[13] – with the same opening progression: Example 24.

The message of *Winter*, however, is that man can shrug off, smile at and even enjoy Nature's taunts. Much of the first movement is constructed in rhythms that convey, like lines 1 and 4 of the sonnet, both the cold and people's physical reaction to it. There is a unity of purposes here: the cold, becoming more intense, progressively induces greater animation in a person. Thus, as the wind has its effect, the initial reiterated quavers become semiquavers for the stamping of feet (bars 20–6) and demisemiquavers for the chattering of teeth (bars 47–55) – not to be confused with demisemiquavers elsewhere that represent winds. In another realization of 'progressive ritornello form', the

Example 24   *Farnace* RV 711, 'Gelido in ogni vena' (Act II scene 6)

powerful sequential consequent is reserved until bar 22 – when it can show the stamping of feet to be the consequence of the cold. By emerging as the dominant element, it claims the right, as it were, to bring the movement to its close.

There can be few musical experiences as satisfying as hearing the slow movement begin: Example 25a. The dark warmth of E♭ major is the perfect welcome, quickly bringing us indoors and shutting out F minor's grey chill. The aria-like melody (considered in Chapter 5) is of undeniable charm, the onomatopoeia of raindrops a nice touch. (In the field of opera, Vivaldi employs pizzicato strings to represent *pioggia di lagrime*, the 'rain of tears'.)[14] But what contributes most to the tableau's affection of smugness and reassurance is the soothing mesh of all the figurations together: a therapeutic rhythm functioning like the murmurings in *Spring* that lull the goatherd to sleep. A useful comparator is the slow movement for recorder, violin and bassoon in the chamber concerto RV 94 (Example 25b). Lacking textural depth, it is less satisfying than its model in *Winter* and thus gives an insight into the extraordinary care that Vivaldi had lavished on the *Seasons*.

The finale's detailed depiction of what it is like to walk and skate on ice might today seem less than impressive. Modern listeners used to the aesthetics of more recent composition can find such frankness – as legs splay apart and the ice cracks (bars 85–93/166–74), for instance – disarmingly simple and apparently lacking in subtlety. The same reception must often be the fate of other pictorial music such as Handel's treatment of images like 'the mountain nods' or 'the forest shakes' (*Acis and Galatea*, 1717). Even the very idea of concentrating on an innocent pastime of ordinary folk might offend those who have too narrow a view of what is valuable in Western art-music: 'Winter, yes – but *skating*?'

But skating was brilliantly chosen, for it symbolizes people's freedom when they live in harmony with nature, and when they are not afraid to take a risk.

Example 25   (a) *Winter*, II (viola part omitted); (b) RV 94, II

Because it is amusing, it also enabled Vivaldi to give freedom to his technique in an easily tolerated, self-effacing way: he too took a risk. And so we should not be deceived by his depictions, but rather marvel at the timelessness of the atmosphere created 'in notes with many a winding bout of linkèd sweetness long drawn out'. Travelling in wide, mesmeric sweeps, the slow progress to the dominant of the dominant (bar 73/154) is achieved with the same hanging inevitability as that of the skater's impending accident. The harmony is static, as if time stands still, and a formal framework is scarcely required. Nowhere else in Op. 8 (except, perhaps, the finale of *Summer*) is ritornello form implemented so freely that its functions are transcended. When the winds come, Sirocco ironically has the rhythm and motivic substance of the opening of *Summer* but none of his former malevolence; now in E♭ major, his gentle warmth recalls the comfort evoked in the slow movement. After that moment of reconciliation, the subsequent battle of winds can do no harm: 'This is winter, but of a kind to bring joy', reads the sonnet. Joy indeed. Who can fail to be moved by the unnerving hint of alarm in the long chromatic manoeuvre over the pedal's hard, dry surface (bars 62–73/143–54) or fail to share in the exhilaration of the ending?

Milton's texts, through a process of transmission that has yet to be uncovered, provided a basis for the programme of *Winter* but not its content, wrapped up in a view of music that is an ideal, not its realization. In dealing with a subject that he had to puzzle out for himself, Vivaldi liberated his art from the chains of convention and discovered something of 'the hidden soul of harmony'.

Notes

1 One collection, two Vivaldis

1 Including arrangements but discounting re-releases. I am indebted to Roger-Claude Travers for communicating this information in private correspondence. The earliest recordings of Vivaldi's music, from 1924 to the early 1950s, are reviewed in R.-C. Travers and T. Walker, 'Discographie Vivaldi 78 tours', *ISV*, 3 (1982), pp. 74–97. Molinari's interpretation (Orchestra dell'Accademia di S. Cecilia, Rome, 1942) was re-released on CD by Ermitage (Salvioni G. & C., Bologna) in 1991: ERM 116S.

2 For obvious practical reasons, this handbook contains no discography; recommendations of particular recordings are given in the Preface. For full listings updated annually, with critical reviews, see R.-C. Travers, 'Discographie Vivaldi', in the volumes of *ISV* (from 1980).

3 An ideal introduction to this recent history is Chapter 1 in Talbot, *Vivaldi*.

4 The earliest modern transcription of the *Seasons* is one for four hands at the piano by Alceo Toni (1919). This and other information on the reception of the *Seasons* is given in C. Vitali, 'Avventure antiche e moderne delle Stagioni vivaldiane', pp. 22–6 in *Symphonia*, supplement to No. 12 (1991): a booklet published with the Ermitage CD cited in note 1.

5 For a review of early modern editions of Vivaldi, illustrated with sample pages from the transcriptions of the *Seasons* by Molinari (Ricordi, 1927), see C. Fertonani, 'Edizioni e revisioni vivaldiane in Italia nella prima metà del novecento (1919–1943)', *Chigiana*, 41, new series 21 (1989), pp. 235–66.

6 The paucity of modern editions of the concertos of Op. 8 other than *The Four Seasons* is a case in point (see Preface). New editions of the *Seasons* are due to appear shortly in the *Nuova edizione critica delle opere di Antonio Vivaldi* (Ricordi, from 1982), the successor to the *Opere strumentali*.

7 For a fuller review of the issues concerning Vivaldi's music in France, see Mamy, '"Le Printemps" d'Antonio Vivaldi'.

8 *Gazette d'Amsterdam*, 14 December 1725.

9 See M. Talbot, 'Vivaldi and a French ambassador', *ISV*, 2 (1981), pp. 31–43.

10 The report (*Mercure de France*, October 1725, pp. 2417–18) is quoted in full in P. Everett and M. Talbot, 'Homage to a French king. Two serenatas by Vivaldi (Venice, 1725 and ca. 1726)', the prefatory essay to Antonio Vivaldi, *Due serenate* ['Wedding Serenata', RV 687, and *La Senna festeggiante*, RV 693], facsimile (Drammaturgia Musicale Veneta 15, Milan, 1995), p. lxviii.

11 Reported in the *Mercure de France*, December 1730, p. 2758.

12 Information in this paragraph is drawn from the catalogue of performances in C. Pierre, *Histoire du Concert spirituel, 1725–1790* (Paris, 1975).

13 See P. Lescat, ' "Il pastor fido", un œuvre de Nicolas Chédeville', *ISV*, 11 (1990), pp. 5–10, and the same writer's paper of the same title in *Vivaldi. Vero e falso. Problemi d'attribuzione*, ed. A. Fanna and M. Talbot (Florence, 1992), pp. 109–26.

14 Title-page: *LE PRINTEMS / ou / LES SAISONS / AMUSANTES / CONCERTOS / DANTONIO VIVALDY / Mis pour Les Musettes et Vielles / avec accompagnement de Violon / Fluste et Basse continue. / PAR Mr CHEDEVILLE LE CADET / Hautbois De la Chambre du Roy / et Musette ordinaire De l'Academie Royalle / De Musique. / OPERA OTTAVA. / Grave par La Basse. / [. . .] / A PARIS / Chez Mr Chedeville [. . .] / Madame Boivin Marchande [. . .] / Le S.^r Le Clerc Marchand [. . .] / AVEC PRIVILEGE DU ROY*. Details of the correlation between the arrangements and Vivaldi's movements are given in Pincherle, *Antonio Vivaldi et la musique instrumentale*, vol. I, p. 223, and in Lescat, '"Il pastor fido"' (1992), p. 123. Chédeville's royal privilege, granted on 7 August 1739, permitted him to make and publish further arrangements of music by Vivaldi and several other specified Italian composers. The project appears to have been abandoned very quickly, however; besides *Le printems ou les saisons amusantes*, only an arrangement of Felice Dall'Abaco's *Sonate da camera* was printed, also in 1739.

15 Corrette's work is scored for two flutes, one oboe, two horns, bassoon, strings, continuo (with organ), vocal soloists and five-part choir. Title-page: *Laudate / Dominum de Coelis. / Psaume 148. / Motet à Grand Choeur / arrangé dans le Concerto / du Printems / de Vivaldi. / Par M^r. Corrette / On peut exécuter ce Motet en Trio, Dessus, Haute-contre, et Basse-Taille. / [. . .] / A Paris aux adresses ordinaires de Musique / et Chez l'Auteur [. . .] / Et à Lyon*. Corrette also drew upon the *Seasons* for some of the examples in his treatise *L'art du violon* (1782). The title-page of Rousseau's arrangement reads: *LE / PRINTEMS / DE / VIVALDI / arrangé pour une Flute / sans accompagnement / PAR / M. J. J. ROUSSEAU / en 1775. / [. . .] / A PARIS / Chez BIGNON, Place du Louvre [. . .]*.

16 *Commedie*, vol. XIII (Venice, 1761), p. 11: *Questo famosissimo Suonator di Violino, quest'uomo celebre per le sue sonate, specialmente per quelle intitolate le* quattro stagioni, *componeva altresì delle Opere in Musica; e quantunque dicessero i buoni Conoscitori, ch'egli mancava nel contrappunto, e che non metteva i Bassi a dovere, faceva cantar bene le parti, e il più delle volte le Opere sue hanno avuto fortuna.*

17 Published anonymously by Pinelli (Venice); ed. G. A. Caula (Studia et Documenta Historiae Musicae 3, Turin, 1965). Excerpts translated into English appear in *Source Readings in Music History*, ed. O. Strunk (New York, 1950).

2 Origin and motivation

1 *Gazette d'Amsterdam*, 14 December 1725.

2 For critical analysis of this and other portraits of the composer, see F. Farges and M. Ducastel-Delacroix, 'Au suget du vrai visage de Vivaldi: essai iconographique', in *Vivaldi. Vero e falso. Problemi d'attribuzione*, ed. A. Fanna and M. Talbot (Florence, 1992), pp. 159–70.

3 In the present translation of the title-page, Václav Morzin's name and lands are given in their German forms, following the style of the print itself – German being the administrative language of eighteenth-century Bohemia. Hohen Elbe (also spelt 'Hohenelbe') is the German name for the north Bohemian town known today as Vrchlabí. The Czech equivalents of Lomnitz, Tschista, Krzinetz and Kaunitz are Lomnice, Čistá, Křinec and Kounice, respectively. Doubek and Sowoluska do not appear to match any modern Czech place-names.

4 Counts Ferdinand Maximillian Franz von Morzin (?–1763) and Karl Joseph Franz von Morzin (1717–83).

5 *I–Tn*, Foà 32, ff. 103–10; see note 20. A few markings such as 'M.' on certain other autograph scores preserved in Turin might conceivably stand for 'Morzin', but alternative interpretations are possible. See P. Everett, 'Vivaldi's marginal markings: clues to sets of instrumental works and their chronology', in *Irish Musical Studies. 1: Musicology in Ireland*, ed. G. Gillen and H. White (Dublin, 1990), pp. 248–63: 258–60.

6 Talbot, 'Vivaldi and the Empire', p. 36.

7 Heller, *Antonio Vivaldi*, pp. 190–1 and 406.

8 Talbot, 'Vivaldi and the Empire', pp. 37–41.

9 The minute of the decision taken on 2 July by the governors of the Pietà – preserved in the Archivio di Stato, Venice: Ospedali e luoghi pii diversi, Busta 691, Notatorio N.1, f. 179 – is reproduced and transcribed in Giazotto, *Antonio Vivaldi*, pp. 256 and 374.

10 Talbot, *Vivaldi*, p. 167.

11 The Manchester sources for the *Seasons* are discussed in Everett, *Manchester Concerto Partbooks*, pp. 222–33, and 'Vivaldi concerto manuscripts in Manchester: I'; the latter includes reproductions of selected pages. The dating of the manuscripts and further evidence of their authority are reported in P. Everett, 'Vivaldi's Italian copyists', *ISV*, 11 (1990), pp. 27–88: 53 and 65–6; and P. Everett and M. Talbot, 'Homage to a French king. Two serenatas by Vivaldi (Venice, 1725 and ca. 1726)', the prefatory essay to Antonio Vivaldi, *Due serenate* ['Wedding Serenata', RV 687, and *La Senna festeggiante*, RV 693], facsimile (Drammaturgia Musicale Veneta 15, Milan, 1995), p. xxxix.

12 Everett, 'Vivaldi concerto manuscripts in Manchester: I', pp. 33–4. The Lund manuscript is of Swedish provenance, not German as stated there.

13 In this context the term 'organo' does not signify only an organ, although an organ may be used in the continuo group.

14 Like many Italian composers, Vivaldi typically added figures to his manuscripts only sparsely or not at all; he could expect experienced players to realize the harmony without help. The publisher could have no such expectation when the bass was presented as a separate part and when many customers were amateur musicians; he would therefore ensure that figures were edited in as necessary. Figures appear in the autograph scores concordant with works in Op. 8 (see Plate 3), but they are fewer than those in the print and not always the same.

15 Page '10*', inserted between pp. 10 and 11 of the part; see Everett, 'Vivaldi concerto manuscripts in Manchester: I', pp. 37–8, 44 and 48. An incomplete copy of the Le Cène edition recently sold at Sotheby's (1 December 1994, Lot 384) revealed that the page is inscribed *en reliant ce livre il faut que cette feui[lle] reste detaché* ('when binding this fascicle, this folio must stay detached').

16 The other concertos called *La tempesta di mare* are RV 98, 433 and 570. In F major, they are musically related to each other but not directly to RV 253.

17 Probably 'the favourite concerto . . . by Vivaldi' advertised in London on 21 December 1717; see Ryom, *Répertoire*, pp. 37–8 and 421–3. Confusion over the identity of the bird is evident – a different version of the work, RV 335a, is called *Il rosignuolo* ('The Nightingale') – but no source indicating Vivaldi's preference survives.

18 Everett, 'Towards a Vivaldi chronology', pp. 752–4.

19 *Ibid.*, pp. 755–6, and Everett, 'Vivaldi's marginal markings' (see note 5), pp. 258–61. The present writer's discovery of the scores' connections was first reported in M. Talbot, 'Vivaldi in the Sale Catalogue of Nicolaas Selhof', *ISV*, 6 (1985), pp. 57–63: 61. The manuscript of RV 270 carries an alternative title, *Per il S[antissim]o Natale* ('For the Holy Nativity'), added, presumably in reference to a particular performance, after 'Il riposo' had been written.

20 The attribution of RV 90, 104, 129, 151, 271, 496 and 579 to the early and mid-1720s is based on evidence, as yet unpublished, gathered in the present writer's studies of Vivaldi's autograph manuscripts and copy-manuscripts he possessed. Evidence for the dating of RV 95, 294, 544 and 572 is given in Everett, 'Vivaldi concerto manuscripts in Manchester: II'. To this list might be added two other works known to date from the same period, although they are not allusive or characterized concertos in the same general sense: the title of *Amato bene* (RV 761) relates to the aria by Vivaldi on which the concerto's slow movement is loosely based, and *L'ottavina* (RV 763) was so-named in reference to the concerto's solo passages played an octave higher than notated. At later dates, Vivaldi made new versions of *Il gardellino* (as RV 428) and *La notte* (RV 439 and 501).

21 Only the composer's deleted inscription survives, on a leaf (f. 110) later used for the autograph of RV 496: see notes 5 and 20.

22 P. Everett, 'Towards a chronology of Vivaldi manuscripts', *ISV*, 8 (1987), pp. 90–106: 97. The work itself and the issues it raises are discussed in M. Talbot, 'Vivaldi's Conch Concerto', *ISV*, 5 (1984), pp. 66–82.

23 On these manuscripts and their history, see Everett, *Manchester Concerto Partbooks*, pp. 123–222 and 437–44, and 'Vivaldi concerto manuscripts in Manchester: I' and '. . . II'.

24 Their existence, as manuscripts, was documented in 1759; see Talbot, 'Vivaldi in the Sale Catalogue of Nicolaas Selhof', pp. 60–1. The example called 'Il Gran Mogul' may have been connected in some way with the violin concerto RV 208, which, in a Schwerin manuscript, is entitled 'Grosso Mogul'.

25 Heller, *Die deutsche Überlieferung*, pp. 24, 27, 51, 93 and 202.

26 Two of the parts' handwritings are those of scribes '3' and '4' who are known to have worked with the composer. Scribe 4 is believed to be Giovanni Battista Vivaldi (1655–1736), Antonio's father. Everett, 'Vivaldi's Italian copyists' (see note 11), pp. 33–7 and 49–53.

27 The basis for this conclusion is Vivaldi's use of particular music-papers for a group of manuscripts that includes works dedicated to persons connected with the composer's residence in Mantua. Everett, 'Towards a Vivaldi chronology', pp. 752–4.

28 Everett, 'Vivaldi concerto manuscripts in Manchester: II', pp. 20–3 and 50–1, and *Manchester Concerto Partbooks*, pp. 198–208. The principal evidence for this conclusion concerns a passage grafted into a solo episode in the finale, a revision probably made especially for Op. 8: bars 223–41/331–49.

29 Heller, *Die deutsche Überlieferung*, pp. 15–22 and 77. The fourth page of the manuscript is reproduced on p. 53.

30 Everett, 'Towards a Vivaldi chronology', pp. 752–4.

31 Heller, *Die deutsche Überlieferung*, p. 94.

32 This second state of RV 210 is reflected in the parts of German provenance preserved at Schwerin, a source described *ibid.*, p. 173.

33 An impression created when Vivaldi is seen to have used a limited batch of one variety of music-paper (defined according to both paper-type and rastrography) for few compositions. The basis for such conclusions is discussed in Everett, 'Towards a Vivaldi chronology'.

34 Talbot, *Vivaldi*, p. 167.

35 An initiative revealed in a letter dated 11 November 1724 from Vivaldi to Count Carlo Giacinto Roero di Guarene, reported in M. Talbot, 'The fortunes of Vivaldi biography, from Pincherle to the present', *Chigiana*, 41, new series 21 (1989), pp. 113–35: 129.

36 In the case of Vivaldi's Op. 2 sonatas, the music was in the press even before the dedicatee was chosen: Talbot, *Vivaldi*, p. 35. It is likely, however, that Morzin was the intended candidate for Op. 8 from the outset, for Vivaldi could not have considered dedicating to another patron music already given to the count.

3 Ritornello forms

1 'Herrn Johann Joachim Quantzens Lebenslauf, von ihm selbst entworfen', in F. W. Marpurg, *Historisch-kritische Beyträge zur Aufnahme der Musik*, vol. I (Berlin, 1754–5), pp. 197–250: 205.

2 The Ricordi edition is faulty at this point: the bass part given for bars 12–13/183–4 belongs to bars 11–12. The error arises from the original *organo e violoncello* part, which gives, as consecutive bars, tenor-clef and bass-clef versions of bar 11 at the higher and lower octaves and only three bars rest for the next phrase.

3 The Ricordi edition incorrectly has the full continuo group entering only at bar 16/175 after a cello solo. In both the Le Cène print and the autograph manuscript of RV 210 no such differentiation is made; the bass entry from bar 9/168 is intended for the whole *basso*.

4 The note $c\#^2$ is avoided, as if the second violins are limited to the harmonic series of D.

5 Talbot, 'The concerto Allegro', p. 170. Talbot notes Vivaldi's custom of indicating with a *da capo* direction that the final ritornello repeats the first. In some cases the marking was later

converted to a *dal segno* arrangement, requiring a repeat of only the last part of the first ritornello. The autographs concordant with Op. 8 Nos. 7–11 hint, however, that Vivaldi had not yet begun to take this notational short cut regularly; the final period in each movement is written out, even when a *dal segno* marking would have produced the same result, as if the option of reusing the first period was simply not entertained.

6 A German term meaning 'heraldic device', coined by Hugo Riemann (*Handbuch der Musikgeschichte* (Berlin,1922)), that refers to a process in which the soloist's opening passage is interrupted by part of the ritornello before being allowed, at it were, to restart and proceed.

7 Vivaldi's willingness to reconsider the *tutti* framework prior to compiling Op. 8 is demonstrated by his adaptation, in the autograph, of the second ritornello of the finale: the deletion of a seven-bar phrase falling between bars 76/247 and 77/248 that exactly reproduced, in G minor, bars 17–23/188–94.

8 Talbot (*Vivaldi*, p. 78) draws attention to a case concerning the finale of Op. 9 No. 10 (RV 300).

9 Examples include the first movements of RV 336 and RV 391.

10 It appears, for instance, in the first movement of RV 246, a work dating from *c*. 1720.

4 Expression and meaning

1 *The Art of Playing on the Violin* (London, 1751; facsimile ed. David D. Boyden (London, 1952)), p. 1.

2 *Ibid.*: 'As the imitating [of] the Cock, Cuckoo, Owl, and other Birds; or the Drum, French Horn, Tromba-Marina, and the like . . . rather belong to the Professors of Legerdemain and Posture-masters than to the Art of Musick, the Lovers of that Art are not to expect anything of that sort in this Book.' Boyden (*The History of Violin Playing*, p. 337) observes that these words were not included in the French translation published in Paris *c*. 1752, having presumably been omitted for fear of offending French musicians' preference for this kind of depiction.

3 An anonymous *Lettre sur la musique française en réponse à celle de Jean-Jacques Rousseau*, quoted in English translation in Pincherle, *Vivaldi: Genius of the Baroque*, p. 199.

4 *Ibid.*, pp. 182–200.

5 Especially Fertonani, *Antonio Vivaldi. La simbologia musicale*. See also Zoppelli, 'Tempeste e Stravaganze'; Cross, *The Late Operas of Antonio Vivaldi*; and R. Strohm, *Giustino by Antonio Vivaldi. Introduction, Critical Notes and Critical Commentary* (Milan, 1992).

6 Fertonani, *Antonio Vivaldi. La simbologia musicale*, provides a comprehensive review of programmatic and allusively titled instrumental music of the seventeenth and eighteenth centuries. See also Ringer, 'The *Chasse* as a musical topic', and Boyden, *The History of Violin Playing*.

7 Modern edition of Biber's sonata (in A major, for violin and continuo): ed. Nikolaus Harnoncourt (Diletto Musicale 372, Vienna and Munich, 1977).

8 Fertonani, *Antonio Vivaldi. La simbologia musicale*, p. 50.

9 Described *ibid.*, pp. 119–20.

10 Another case is Vivaldi's appending of the words *Il Proteò ò sia* ('Proteus or') to the original title of the concerto RV 544, *Il Mondo al rovescio* ('The World Upside-Down'); see Everett, 'Vivaldi concerto manuscripts in Manchester: II', pp. 29–33.

11 The Le Cène print and the Ricordi edition are faulty at bar 249/357. Manuscript concordances in Manchester and Dresden show that the note f^2 was intended in the principal part (double-stopped with $b\flat^1$), which completes the four-note descent from $b\flat^2$ in bar 247/355.

12 Likewise, bird-song at the beginning of *Pleasure* (from bar 15) is symbolic of the work's agreeableness. Fertonani, *Antonio Vivaldi. La simbologia musicale*, p. 146.

13 Pincherle (*Vivaldi: Genius of the Baroque*, pp. 144–5) provides statistics of the distribution of tonic keys for 480 concertos and sinfonias. A more complete view may be gained from Ryom, *Répertoire*.

14 Several examples of agitated arias in G minor, with affections such as 'fear' and 'revenge', are discussed in Cross, *The Late Operas of Antonio Vivaldi*, pp. 65–6, 69–70, 76, 97 and 136.

15 Strohm (*Giustino by Antonio Vivaldi*, pp. 51–6) distinguishes between keys in the opera *Giustino* that are used frequently – and thus apparently without dramatic significance – and 'characteristic' and 'individual' keys that seem to be associated (with related imagery) with particular characters or the relationships between characters. He concludes (p. 53): 'the individualisation by key is somehow analogous to the social and dramatic hierarchy of the roles'.

16 Heinichen's treatise (Dresden, 1728) is translated in G. J. Buelow, *Thorough-Bass Accompaniment According to Johann David Heinichen* (Berkeley and Los Angeles, 1966). On Heinichen's views in relation to those of Mattheson, Marpurg and Quantz, see R. Steblin, *A History of Key Characteristics in the Eighteenth and Early Nineteenth Centuries* (Ann Arbor, 1983), pp. 55–6, 80 and 95.

17 Transcriptions of the aria settings are given in G. J. Buelow, 'The *Loci Topici* and affect in late Baroque music: Heinichen's practical demonstration', *The Music Review*, 27 (1966), pp. 161–76.

5 The slow movements

1 In the Le Cène print the slow movement of No. 9 is for the principal violin (or oboe) and *basso continuo* only: a scoring given also in the autograph manuscript of the work. The Ricordi edition is faulty not only in showing the use of violas; unaccountably, it also omits many original and valid bass figures, suppresses the use of crotchets in the bass part in bar 7, and changes certain pitches of the bass and the rhythm of the solo part in bar 2.

2 Transcribed in M. Talbot, *Tomaso Albinoni: the Venetian Composer and His World* (Oxford, 1990), p. 54.

3 It is a 'recitative of anguish' according to Pincherle (*Vivaldi: Genius of the Baroque*, p. 185), who refers to the description of the movement by Schering (*Geschichte des Instrumentalkonzerts*, p. 93): 'a kind of *lamento* of the castaways'.

4 Another case is the central *Recitativo sostenuto* of a violin concerto in C minor by Mauro d'Alai, a work markedly Vivaldian in style; see Everett, *The Manchester Concerto Partbooks*, pp. 292–3. Like the syllabic setting of a vocal text, the solo part is notated in separately flagged quavers and semiquavers.

5 See pp. 80, 86, 87 and 97 regarding *The Four Seasons*. Cases of borrowing are instanced in Ryom, *Répertoire*; Cross, *The Late Operas of Antonio Vivaldi*; E. Cross, 'Vivaldi's operatic borrowings', *Music and Letters*, 59 (1978), pp. 429–39; K. Kropfinger, 'Vivaldi as self-borrower', in *Opera and Vivaldi*, ed. M. Collins and E. K. Kirk (Austin, 1984), pp. 308–26; and other writings.

6 'Bel piacer di fido core' (*Allegro non molto*, 3/8 metre), from Act II scene 8 of *L'Atenaide* RV 702, is a very similar case.

7 *Die Violinkonzerte Giuseppe Tartinis als Ausdruck einer Künstlerpersönlichkeit und einer Kulturepoche* (Wolfenbüttel, 1935; 2nd edn 1966). All captions are given in the book's catalogue of the violin concertos.

8 'Tartini, Giuseppe', in *The New Grove Dictionary of Music and Musicians*, ed. S. Sadie, 20 vols. (London, 1980), vol. 18, pp. 583–8: 586.

9 I am grateful to Michael Talbot for drawing my attention to this case. Modern edition of D12: ed. E. Farina (Milan, 1975).

6 *The Four Seasons*

1 This is an aspect covered thoroughly elsewhere, particularly in Boyden, *The History of Violin Playing*, and the writings of Pincherle.

2 See Cross, *The Late Operas of Antonio Vivaldi*, pp. 57–8, 71, 98, 100–1 and 123.

3 Since Venetian dialect does not use double consonants, local writers employing standard Italian (Tuscan) often 'hypercorrected' – making single consonants double.

4 Their texts differ from the versions given in the Manchester manuscripts only in minor respects.

5 Everett, 'Vivaldi concerto manuscripts in Manchester: I', p. 33.

6 The subject also of his English sonnet *To the Nightingale* (*c.* 1629).

7 Research on this aspect is incomplete, having begun when I stumbled on the Milton connection only weeks before the present book went to press. Nevertheless, it seemed imperative to include here a matter that causes a fundamental revision in our understanding of the *Seasons*. A major article on the subject is in preparation.

8 Entitled 'La Fortuna in macchina' (Act I scene 5). The music was again reused, this time in C major, for both the sinfonia and the first chorus in *Dorilla in Tempe* RV 709 – at least in the opera's production of 1734 (for which a score is extant), if not also in earlier productions (from 1726).

9 The version of the Manchester manuscripts gives four lightning flashes (one on each beat), not two. Everett, 'Vivaldi concerto manuscripts in Manchester: I', pp. 38 and 51.

10 Deryck Cooke (*The Language of Music* (London, 1959), p. 163) attributes to it 'an incoming painful emotion, an acceptance of, or yielding to grief; passive suffering; and the despair connected with death'.

11 These and several other 'sleep' contexts in Vivaldi's music are assessed in Fertonani, *Antonio Vivaldi. La simbologia musicale*, pp. 107–9.

12 An adaptation of the arioso appears in Act II scene 8 of *Griselda* RV 718 (1735).

13 *Siroe, re di Persia* RV 735 (1727), Act III scene 5. The music of this opera is lost, but the setting in question was presumably the same as the extant version for the 1731 production of *Farnace* RV 711 (Act II scene 6).

14 *Giustino* RV 717 (1724), Act II scene 1: aria, 'Sento in seno ch'in pioggia di lagrime'.

Select bibliography

Boyden, David D. *The History of Violin Playing from its Origins to 1761 and its Relationship to the Violin and Violin Music* (London, 1965).

Braun, Werner. *Antonio Vivaldi. Concerti grossi, op. 8, Nr. 1–4. Die Jahreszeiten* (Munich, 1975).

Burrows, David. 'Style in culture: Vivaldi, Zeno and Ricci', *The Journal of Interdisciplinary History*, 4 (1973–4), pp. 1–23.

Cross, Eric. *The Late Operas of Antonio Vivaldi 1717–1738*, 2 vols. (Ann Arbor, 1981).

Eller, Rudolf. 'Geschichtliche Stellung und Wandlung der Vivaldischen Konzertform', in *Bericht über den Internationalen Musikwissenschaftlichen Kongress Wien 1956* (Graz and Cologne, 1958), pp. 150–5.

Everett, Paul. 'Vivaldi concerto manuscripts in Manchester: I', ' . . . II' and ' . . . III', *ISV*, 5 (1984), pp. 23–52; 6 (1985), pp. 3–56; and 7 (1986), pp. 5–34.

'Towards a Vivaldi chronology', in *Nuovi studi vivaldiani. Edizione e cronologia critica delle opere*, ed. A. Fanna and G. Morelli (Florence, 1988), pp. 729–57.

The Manchester Concerto Partbooks, 2 vols. (New York and London, 1989).

Fertonani, Cesare. *Antonio Vivaldi. La simbologia musicale nei concerti a programma* (Pordenone, 1992).

Giazotto, Remo. *Antonio Vivaldi* (Turin, 1973).

Heller, Karl. *Die deutsche Überlieferung der Instrumentalwerke Vivaldis* (Leipzig, 1971).

Antonio Vivaldi (Leipzig, 1991).

Hutchings, Arthur. *The Baroque Concerto* (London, 1959; 3rd edn, 1973).

Kolneder, Walter. *Antonio Vivaldi: Leben und Werk* (Wiesbaden, 1965). English translation by Bill Hopkins: *Antonio Vivaldi: his Life and Work* (London, 1970).

'Musikalische Symbolik bei Vivaldi', in *Vivaldi veneziano europeo*, ed. F. Degrada (Florence, 1980), pp. 13–23.

'"Laudate Dominum", eine Motette von Michel Corrette nach dem Frülingskonzert op. VIII n. 1 von Vivaldi', in *Logos Musicae. Festschrift für A. Palm*, ed. R. Görner (Wiesbaden, 1982), pp. 124–30.

'The solo concerto', in *Concert Music (1630–1750)*, ed. G. Abraham, The New Oxford History of Music 6 (Oxford and New York, 1986), pp. 302–76.

Mamy, Sylvie. '"Le Printemps" d'Antonio Vivaldi revu et corrigé à Paris par Nicolas Chédeville, Michel Corrette et Jean–Jacques Rousseau', *ISV*, 13 (1992), pp. 51–65.

Orrey, Leslie. *Programme Music: a Brief Survey from the Sixteenth Century to the Present Day* (London, 1975).

Pincherle, Marc. *Antonio Vivaldi et la musique instrumentale*, 2 vols. (Paris, 1948).

Vivaldi (Paris, 1955). English translation by Christopher Hatch: *Vivaldi: Genius of the Baroque* (New York, 1957; reprinted London, 1958).

Ringer, Alexander L. 'The *Chasse* as a musical topic of the 18th century', *Journal of the American Musicological Society*, 4 (1953), pp. 148–59.

Ryom, Peter. *Répertoire des Œuvres d'Antonio Vivaldi. Les compositions instrumentales* (Copenhagen, 1986).

Schering, Arnold. *Geschichte des Instrumentalkonzerts bis auf der Gegenwart* (Leipzig, 1905; 2nd edn, 1927).

Selfridge-Field, Eleanor. *Venetian Instrumental Music from Gabrieli to Vivaldi* (Oxford, 1975).

Talbot, Michael. 'The concerto Allegro in the early eighteenth century', *Music and Letters*, 52 (1971), pp. 8–18 and 159–72.

Vivaldi (London, 1978; 2nd edn, 1993).

'Vivaldi's Four Seasons', *Music Teacher*, 59 (1980), pp. 16–18.

'Vivaldi and the Empire', *ISV*, 8 (1987), pp. 31–51.

Antonio Vivaldi: a Guide to Research (New York and London, 1988). Revised, in Italian translation, as *Vivaldi: fonti e letteratura critica* (Florence, 1991).

Zoppelli, Luca. 'Tempeste e Stravaganze: fattori estetici e ricettivi in margine alla datazione dei concerti "a programma"', in *Nuovi studi vivaldiani. Edizione e cronologia critica delle opere*, ed. A. Fanna and G. Morelli (Florence, 1988), pp. 801–10.

Index

DATE DUE

#47-0108 Peel Off Pressure Sensitive